Open House:
Debunking the Myth of the "Happy Homeowner"

Published by 1840Publishing LLC; 1840Media LLC Group (USA)

First publication: December, 2015

Ebook Publication: November, 2015

Copyright © Jesse Green 2014, 2015, 2016

Copyrighted images used with permission or under license

All Rights Reserved

1840Media LLC™

Library of Congress Cataloging-in-Publication date has been applied for

ISBN: 978-0-9966022-1-1

Published in the United States of America

Edited by Rebecca Adams Wright (though she tried to warn us.)

Layout by 1840Media LLC

Without limiting rights under copyright reserved above, no part of this publication maybe reproduced, stored in or introduced into a retrieval system, or transmitted, in order, or by any other means without the prior written permission of both the copyright owner and the publisher of this book.

Please be kind and support the authors' rights.

Dedication

To my lovely, brilliant and amazingly patient wife who keeps our lives from derailing and forces me to eat occasionally when I'm writing; and to my multi-talented son, a young Renaissance man who never ceases to make me proud, though I don't remember to tell him often enough. Wait, my wife says I also have to write that she provided inimitable support during the grueling process of making bad real estate jokes and without her the book would never have been written. Yes, dear.

Much appreciation to my "real author" friend David, Dan, who thinks my snotty comments are funny and various supportive friends and relatives. I'd never have finished this project without all of your transparently phony compliments and encouragement.
This is your fault too.

Thanks to Becky who took on the job of editing even though, I'm sure, this project seemed like the sort of thing that might ruin her career. Any good to be found here is likely her doing and all poor grammar, typos, bad decisions about content and other mistakes are entirely my fault for ignoring her good advice.

Also, grudging appreciation for all the shyster house-pushers I've battled over the years. If you had not sufficiently angered and frustrated me I'd have never been motivated enough to write this book.
Thanks. No, wait. Screw you. I hope this pisses you off.

About The Author

Jesse Green claims to have been building, rebuilding, remodeling and renovating houses for decades at various levels of effectiveness. He blames this on his father who, he claims, taught him how to do these things.

Mr Green also claims to be an award wining journalist, and author.

Mr Green doesn't suffer fools gladly or have time for a level.

Mr Green has no ill will toward real estate agents or builders or even loan officers or lobbyists under the theory that we should forgive people rather than allowing well-deserved resentment to fester and ruin breakfast. He refuses to forgive the insurance people though as he believes they are evil incarnate.

Contents

Preface	1
Introduction	3
Houses and Homes	7

Chapter 1
"There's Never Been a Better Time To Buy A House!"	11
The Myth of the Happy Homeowner	12
A Real Life Real Estate Anecdote	17
The "Starter House"	20
The House Financing Industry	21
Your Best Friend, the House Expert	25
House of Cards	26

Chapter 2: No Money for You!
Our Example House	30
What Counts as House Owning Costs?	31
Financing Costs: "The Money Changers"	35
The Tax Man	38
Insurance Costs	39
Replacement, Repair, and Maintenance	40
Replacement Table	44
Replacement Table Notes	45
Repairs and Maintenance	48
Repair and Maintenance Table	50
Maintenance Table Notes	52
Luxury Costs	54
Luxury Cost Table	56
Luxury Cost Table Notes	57
Upgrades: "Spruce Up Your House for Summer!"	58
Lord of the Land	62
Second Mortgages	65
Closing Costs	66

Chapter 3: Where are the Profits?	71
Myth Versus Reality.	75
Mortgage Interest Deductions	76
Property Tax Deduction	79
The Strawmen: Landlords	80
"Ya' Gotta Live Somewhere" (Replacing Rent)	82
The "Locked-In Payment" Argument	86
Rents Increase?	88
House Tally: So Much for "Profit"	89
A Real World Example	92
Chapter 4: No More "Man of the Castle"	103
Neighbors: Fellow Travelers in Hell	106
Chained like a Dog to a Tree	107
The Man	110
Mortgage Holders	111
Insurance ~~Watch~~dogs	114
Utilities and Roads	117
Ordinances (A Parable)	119
Home Owners Associations	123
In The Beginning	126
Conclusion	132

***

Post Script	136
Broken Fourth Wall Note	149

"When one has finally finished building one's house, one suddenly realizes that in the process one has learned something that one really needed to know in the worst way –before one began."

Friedrich Nietzsche

Preface

Sigh. You'll probably go ahead and finance a damned house, no matter what we say.

You'll obtain a thirty-year mortgage. You'll pay PMI, taxes, mandatory insurance, and, eventually, up to double the purchase price in interest. You'll pay more than the house is worth for repairs and upkeep. You'll make payments to layers of intermediaries and third parties. You'll never consider all of the lost opportunities for the time and money you'll tie up in the house. You won't give a thought to how much of your wealth will be committed, years in advance, to watching a backhoe tear up your lawn to replace sewer lines instead of taking your kids to Disney.

No matter how many examples we provide, how many facts and statistics we bring you, the myth of The Happy-Homeowner is all-powerful. Few have the willpower to resist. It's sad, really. Like hearing that certain people are still willing to fund new Adam Sandler movies. There's no rational explanation for some behavior. (Recall what George Carlin said about people.[1])

Still, our hope is that the information in this book might nurture in you some reasonable doubts and hesitation.

Maybe you'll question one goofy claim a real estate agent makes. Maybe you'll pause to wonder if it's a good idea to pawn Granny's wedding ring to make that interest-only mortgage payment. Maybe you'll ask seemingly obvious questions: What happens if my house doesn't appreciate at 11% per year, and my first novel doesn't make me a millionaire before the balloon payment is due, and the crazy neighbor really does have special forces training in how to kill me with one finger, and that huge sinkhole next door does spread?

Could be you'll pause long enough to notice how implausible the layers of "always win" "never lose" "make easy money by just paying my bills" house hyperbole really are. Maybe, just maybe, we can persuade you to notice how bizarre and self-destructive the entire ritual of house buying can be, rather than just blindly doing everything the bank and real estate salesperson tells you to do.

At the very least we hope this book will help you ponder the buying of a house using the same critical thinking skills you bring to bear on similar huge, life-changing, financial decisions like…well. Hmmmmm.

---

[1] *"Think about how dumb the average person is. Now realize, by definition, that means half of them are even dumber than that."* RIP, Mr. Carlin.

See? There's another thing to think about. For most people buying a house is the single largest financial decision of their lives. It's also the one they know the least about.

Whatever you decide, please don't base the single largest financial decision of your life on myths and promises from house-pushing people who stand to make a fortune from you.

Read this amusing, informal, unofficial little guide. Take notes. Then, if you still want to go finance a house, ask questions and do your own research.

Most important of all don't sign one paper or let go of one penny until you have satisfied yourself that you have all the information—accurate information—about what you're getting yourself into.

"I find little evidence that homeowners are happier by any of the following definitions: life satisfaction, overall mood, overall feeling, general moment-to-moment emotions (i.e., affect) and affect at home… They are also more likely to be 12 pounds heavier, report a lower health status and poorer sleep quality. They tend to spend less time on active leisure or with friends. The average homeowner reports less joy from love and relationships… Contrary to popular belief, I do not find significant differences in family-related time use patterns, family-related affect, number of normal work hours, indicators of stress or measures of self-esteem and perceived control of life by homeownership …."
Dr. Grace Wong Bucchianeri, "The American Dream?" Wharton

Introduction

Sixty three percent of United States Census households own their own house.

There are 132,452,405 units of housing in this vast and amazingly diverse nation. That implies a lot of house owners.

Houses support a huge, powerful industry. Actually, they support many: Buying, clearing, and developing land, building residential houses, remodeling and renovating houses, selling houses, fixing houses, marketing do-it-yourself materials directly to house owners, selling services and appliances for houses, and knocking houses down to build more houses.

Think, too, of all the other weird or unlikely businesses that cater to house owners. Invisible fence installers. Gutter cleaners. Alarm companies. Custom blind makers. Driveway pavers and resurfacers. Student Painters. Landscape supply. Lawn care and landscaping services. Snow removal. Pest control. Kitchen and bath centers. Flooring showrooms. Tile outlets.

Each year Americans spend over $500,000,000,000 on houses. That's half a trillion dollars. So it might be more accurate to so say that much of all the industry in America is devoted to houses. That's why The Wall Street Journal and Forbes and other financial monitors obsessively track housing starts and prices. Residential housing is one of the major engines of the U.S. economy.

Your local municipality likely could not function without residential property taxes. Across the United States property taxes are the single largest source of funding for state and local government. So naturally all of the folks in the nearest tax levying authority are very interested in citizens owning houses.

> The real estate, banking and insurance industries are collectively the largest political lobbying group in the USA. In 2013-2014 they spent $498,855,886 on lobbying your elected officials. The construction industry, separately, spent another $65,180,455. Obviously this has _no influence at all_ on current law and policy regarding housing.

Which raises the question: which came first, the myth of the happy and profitable house buyer, or the sizable chunk of the GDP that depends on that myth? The chicken or the egg?

Some folks believe that houses are so inherently nifty that our cultural worship of house owning is to be expected—like a natural fondness for bacon, fuzzy baby animals, or not-being-poked-in-the-eye. In that view, the size and strength of the house-pushing industry is just a natural reflection of the magical, sparkly wonder of house ownership.

Well, some people also believe that sending money to Pastor Joe via PayPal to cure mysterious and painful genital warts makes more sense than real medical attention. Some people believe that it's unpatriotic to question political promises. Some people can be a bit slow.

An academic might stop here to pontificate for pages on the manifold economic factors leading to the current housing climate and our country's dysfunctional cultural attitude toward house ownership. We're taking the slightly different approach of dictating house jokes to an assistant who is drafting text in a fun and playful fashion on an iPad while we sip mimosas at a beach front bar in Cabo San Lucas. We figure most people aren't interested in reading dry jargon-filled academic treatises about housing or everyone would already know all this stuff. We plan to lure you in with our wit and charm and then teach you about houses while your defenses are down. Plus we are going to scare you a bit.

This little book exists because we really care about helping you to make an informed decision about financing (or, better yet, not financing) a house. But it makes no economic difference to us whether you buy a house, rent a house, or live in an abandoned rail car just past where the pavement ends. We (unlike most house information sources) don't have skin in that game. When you compare our information to other information ask yourself: how much money does this bank or real estate person stand to make?

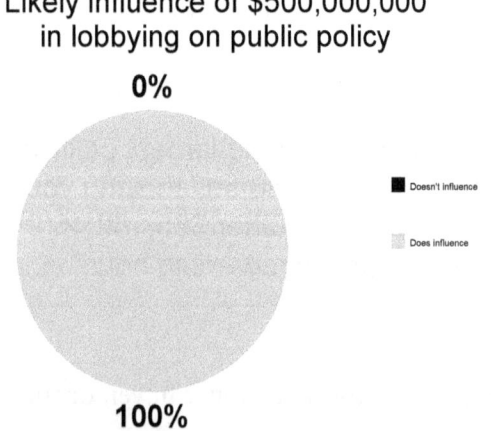

Back to that chicken-or-the-egg question. Considering the dump-truck-loads of money involved, we find it most realistic and entertaining to assume that the vast American housing industry and its equally-vast lobbying efforts just might be influencing our nation's housing decisions.[2] Perhaps. A wee bit.[2] It seem that we might be encouraged to buy houses even though they're usually a terrible deal

---

[2] $498,855,886 plus $65,180,455 is the sum of the house industry lobbying expenditures, remember that from page 3? Our free gas station solar calculator won't even let us add numbers that large.

Introduction

> Throughout this book you'll find thrilling, amazing, allegedly true stories about neighbors sent to us by our loyal readers. Like this one:
>
> My favorite neighbor:
> "Residents in a Charlotte neighborhood say they're fed up with a neighbor they say stands at the front door of his home naked, but police say he's not doing anything illegal.
> People in the Cardinal Glen neighborhood in north Charlotte say the man has been doing this for nearly ten years and on Friday, they called police again.
> "I was out rolling the trash can on Friday and I just happened to look over there and he was standing there buck naked," neighbor Pecolia Threatt said.
> Neighbors say the man just stands there naked at his door several times a week. They're disgusted and fed up. "Because my daughter grew up in this neighborhood. Even this week, when she was home from spring break, she would call me at work and say 'Mom, I'm getting ready to go outside, but let me check if he's out there first'. That's how bad it is in the neighborhood," another neighbor, Adrienna Harris, said.
> Harris says she's called police numerous times over the last ten years to complain, but nothing has been done. A spokeswoman for the Charlotte-Mecklenburg Police Department confirms that officers were called to the home on Friday. "Since it's not a criminal incident, it was documented in the 'call for service' but there's no report."

for house owners. Reprise and emphasis: House buying the conventional way is a spectacularly money-wasting, life-sucking, mistake.

The facts and figures we use throughout the book to support this argument are as accurate and up-to-date as possible. Our examples are honest, representative, and based on verifiable facts. When there's ambiguity in the data we magnanimously skew in favor of the pro-house position; we know we can cut the pie bigger in that direction and still show what a lousy deal house ownership is for almost everyone.

We wrote this book for a United States audience. That doesn't mean our friends in Canada and Ireland and India can't read this and take to heart a good tip or two, or, (more likely) shake their heads and get a good laugh at our expense. It just means that most of the financial process, cultural dysfunction and social pressure we discuss is unique to the U.S. If you don't live here that might give you something to envy (or be thankful for.)

There are also places and situations in this wild patchwork nation that are way out of the norm, and where many of the facts and figures and averages in this book aren't going to be applicable.

People dealing with the madness that's the NYC[3] real estate market are on their own: there's no possible model of that rabbit-hole/house of mirrors that could do it justice. The same goes for people

But where will we obtain *our* house financing information?

---

3 Or Boston, San Fransisco, and similar cities where logic and reality have been forgotten

Introduction

buying a house trailer sitting in the middle of the desert outside El Paso, or off-grid cabins in Michigan's Upper Peninsula.

Navigating these unusual real-estate situations is sort of like driving a car powered by fast food grease: good for you, we wish you luck, but there's a reason the EPA doesn't issue mileage estimates for your garage-cobbled grease vehicle. The logistics of your situation are so far off the curve we can't help you much with our fancy facts and examples. Except maybe by entertaining you and showing you a bit of the mainstream mess you've avoided?

One of the most critical points of this book is that of all the myriad reasons not to buy a house, the most compelling is that houses are really crappy investments. In fact, they're not actually investments at all. For the vast majority of people, owning a house is a significant and debilitating expense.

Either we throw the tax refund into this house, or we take it to Vegas.

Houses cost a lot more than the house-pushing industry will admit. The potential for "profit" is almost total BS and spin. If you took all the money you'd spend on owning a house over thirty years and did almost anything else productive with it, you'd be much better off.

Hey. Wait a minute. That's *three* reasons not to buy a house. Any one of which—more cost, less profit, better financial opportunities elsewhere—would make house ownership a lousy investment.

Taken together, these reasons not to buy make financing a house look more like buying recreational drugs or one of those gold-plated exotic cars. You're free to spend your money on these things but don't try to pretend any of them is a practical "investment." They're luxury goods. Moreover, they're extravagant and often wasteful.

To prove it we use fair, representative facts in this book, and break them down for you. For example: Tens of millions of people have lousy credit, buy crappy houses that need huge infusions of cash, and make wildly irresponsible decisions in financing those houses (and are therefore pretty "average" in their way). But we're not going to use *those* average American consumers as examples. We'll use instead the sort of people house-pushers would call "qualified buyers." We offer these "best case" financing scenarios because we don't need to pad our examples to make a point. Facts are facts. No matter who you are, house owning sucks.

This book is also full of statistics, charts, graphs, references to the law and other information. Such material is accurate (unless it's an obvious joke). As accurate as we could make it. Don't base your thesis entirely on us, but you could likely write a pretty good undergrad essay based on our information. Or at least something for the middle-school newspaper.

We've also included here many relevant anecdotes and stories. Such stories are here to prove a point and to entertain you. Each and every one of them comes from some real person. However—as voters, biblical scholars, police detectives, and parents of teens all over the world have discovered—most stories have a nugget of truth and then some spin. We can't vouch for the proportion of spin versus truth in other people's stories; for example, some of the "My Favorite Neighbor" tales so many have shared with us.

All together gentlemen, say: "truth!"

Luckily, it doesn't matter. They're just here for laughs and emphasis. We've changed some names, locations and other identifying features to protect the guilty and foolish.

The house costs outlined in this book are based upon an eminently fair, realistic, average sort of a house, and a house buyer getting a good deal on both the house and financing under current conditions. Our hypothetical buyer has a blue sky sort of future with no wars, Depressions or extinction events on the horizon. Your future may vary.

Houses and Homes

A quick note about our terminology. You may have noticed that we've been using the terms "house buyer" and "house owner" where most folks would use the terms "home buyer" and "homeowner." The house pushing lobby has tried to steal the word "home" and apply it always and only to houses. Not in this book.

People without a place to live are "homeless." The rest of us

An apartment would be fine, thanks.

have a home, even if it's a boat, an apartment, a condo, a buddy's couch, a dorm room, a barracks bunk, an RV, or our parent's basement. "Home," legally, is your residence. The place you spend most nights. Your "home" address.

In this book we call houses, houses. If you're one of the sixty-three percent of people who own your house and live in it, that's your home. Good for you. For the other thirty-seven percent, your home isn't a house that you own. That's great too. In fact, you may be making a much smarter decision than the people who have chosen to buy and live in a house. That's sort of our point.

Without exception, nothing in this book is meant as individual legal or financial advice. Do we have to tell you that? This is a book that uses a photo of four U.S. presidents laughing to illustrate the concept of most stories being at least partially invented. This is a book created in part with graph-making software intended for elementary school kids. This is a book you bought because the description is funny. Please don't rely on us for your personal financial decisions.

Want advice? Here is advice.[4]

Think for Yourself

Back to our opinions. Since we're making the argument that house ownership sucks, the question then becomes, of course, how much does it suck?

In order to answer this burning question, we need to determine which expenses and miseries can accurately be attributed to (blamed on) owning a house, and which are just part of life. Most of us would agree that closing costs and mortgage interest are costs of owning a house. But moving costs apply to everyone whether they're moving into a rental or buying a house. So the former cost counts toward the financial burden of house ownership and the latter doesn't.

What about the cost of repainting? Many renters can and do repaint. Is repainting a cost of owning a house? Are microwave ovens a house cost because most houses these days have one built in, or a universal cost because most everyone has a microwave oven whether they rent or buy? What about lawn maintenance?

---

[4] Ha! Fooled you! Remember we said that *nothing* in this book is advice! Aren't you paying attention?

The same question arises regarding miseries like pest infestations or horrible neighbors. Renters can have unwelcome critters and sociopaths next door, too.

The difference, of course, is that renters don't have to pay for solving most of these problems. If problems get too far out of hand renters have the freedom to go. Sure, moving can be a real pain. But the pain is a couple orders of magnitude more debilitating for a house owner who's spent a year or two of income on closing costs, a down payment, updates, new appliances, and moving costs.

It's true that leases can be hard for renters to break. But those with a real crisis can likely find a way out. If not, they can walk away. Most people financing a house can't afford to excrete that huge amount of money all over again to buy yet another house while waiting for the first to sell, especially if there is that magnitude of trouble with the first.

Selling a house in order to flee a wacky/violent/scary neighbor can be a nightmare. Who wants to buy the house next door to the people with a huge swastika mowed into their lawn, or the meth-addled 20-something, ex-con son who lives in the basement and steals your mail and the change out of your car?

Yes, house owners can "walk away" too. But foreclosure and bankruptcy can screw up life for years and are a sure fire way to stop someone from financing any more houses in the near future. It's easy to get stuck.

In the real world, people who own a house in such situations often have no option but to make the best of it. Due to the large amounts of money involved, these expenses and problems are uniquely debilitating for a house owner. That's why such expenses and situations count strongly against owning a house.

A major theme of this book is that house-pushers don't always have a close and loving relationship with the truth. A lot of spin and a lot of BS are necessary to convince the average hard-working American family to part with about two fifths of their income over 30 years.

So if we can't trust the advice of the people who want our money (and we can't) where do we get our facts?

For this book, we decided to pit self-interested house industries against one another. After all, to run their huge house-pushing enterprises they must have some actual knowledge of such costs. Even if they won't voluntarily share them for our benefit. With tireless searching we found situations where sharing the real costs _benefit_ the industries involved and in those cases they were very happy to share.

For example: want to know what it will really cost to keep a house from disintegrating? Don't ask the people who want to sell you houses. Ask the people who sell replacements for the disintegrating parts. Or those who insure those parts. Or those who manufacture them. Or those who install them.

House sellers want you to think owning a house is a seamless, package deal, like ordering the newest smart phone or tablet. They want you to pay a premium for this purchase while already thinking about the next one.

But the house builders and fixers want you to envision your house as a very expensive, ongoing project—a family member with a rare and difficult disease. Each month brings another transplant or expensive prescription medication. The house suppliers, on the other hand, want you to view your house as a classic car in restoration; every single part needing to be separately considered, sourced and upgraded with the highest quality replacement available.

Insurance firms have turned disaster probability into a science. They make billions doing this. They are very good at it. So naturally they have vast quantities of handy information about the lifespan and costs of almost everything, including all things house-related.

Government agencies, taxing entities, professional groups, academics and many, many other interested parties all have their agendas, their axes to grind and their positions to advance.

We've taken advantage of all these competing viewpoints to find accurate facts and information for you. Once you get the hang of it you can conduct additional, similar research for yourself.

Chapter 1:
"There's Never Been a Better Time To Buy A House!"

--every real estate person, ever

How true.

Of course, it's equally true to say there's never been a worse time to buy a house. Or to say that there's never been a better time to set your hair on fire.

What does it mean to make the claim "there's never been a better time" to do something self-destructive and foolish? Nothing. Just because someone tells you conditions are right to do a stupid thing, doesn't mean that you ought to do it, or to listen, or that it isn't stupid.

That might be a good working summary of this book: Stop! Don't set your hair on fire!

Unlike igniting your head, our culture really does encourage ordinary people to go into crippling debt for 30 years to finance a house. Everyone is supposed to want one. Indeed, house shopping and house buying are treated as a necessary ritual and a rite of passage. Marrying a pile of boards and plaster is seen as a declaration that you're grown-up, responsible, solid and grounded. Owning a house announces to many people "I have my shit together."

"But," a reader might protest, "don't people make amazing amounts of easy money just by owning houses?"

"Well," this book might respond thoughtfully, "for the most part, no. Except in the case of very savvy experts who understand the terrain and those who can avoid conventional financing, houses are almost always hopeless money pits. Tales of vast profits stem mostly from wishful thinking, misleading television, denial, and bad accounting."

"That's not what I heard," our reader might very well reply. "My uncle's neighbor's cousin bought a house back in 1952 for eleven dollars worth of S & H Green Stamps[5] and sold it last year for thirteen bazillion dollars! And I saw this TV show where

---

[5] S & H Green Stamps were a primitive, pre-computer incarnation of a retail frequent card you earned buying groceries and could trade for ancient kitchen gadgets like waffle fryers and bologna crispers.

I expect a house made of $1,000 bills. What is this crap?

regular people were paid to take a house, paid even more to fix it, and then traded it for a small European country where they established their own monarchy."

This book might sigh in understandable frustration and ask how to verify any of this really happened.

First of all, did the uncle's neighbor's cousin account for all the money he spent on interest, termites, roofs, taxes, lawn care, new water heaters, insurance, replacement sewer lines, windows, appliances, driveway repaving and the like, or the value of the time he spent on all the work, or the potential income he might have made if he had done something else with that money, like buying Warren Buffet when the market was low? Secondly, what network was this house show on? What sort of monarchy was established?

Falling for similar (if less obviously mythical) rose-colored too-good-to-be-true anecdotes is how most of us end up financing a house.

The Myth of the Happy Homeowner

How could you (or people you know and love) have walked into such a meat grinding financial miscalculation? How did this happen? Don't feel bad. Many, many Americans have fallen for this con.

For decades the housing, real estate, home improvement and mortgage industries have spent untold millions of dollars on advertising designed to fool us into believing houses are the very embodiment of safety, stability and status. Your elected government has been a willing and active accomplice.

Recall all the ads you've seen featuring happy people posed in front of meticulously landscaped homes. These actors express the sort of uninhibited joy usually reserved for private adult activities. Such well-honed scientifically crafted advertising has helped hide the truth about houses behind a veil of lies, myths and hype.

Houses have been cleverly packaged to be the new symbol of America. Old symbols are dead. Mom moved to Arizona with her yoga instructor, apple pie is full of Alar and high fructose corn syrup, baseball fields are repurposed for lacrosse, and Chevy went bankrupt. Owning a house now ranks only slightly below dying in battle as evidence of patriotism.

The Myth of the Happy Homeowner

Daddy, please tell me the amazing story of the magical, mystical "investment" that couldn't lose money even when it did!

Even after the meltdown of 2008, houses are portrayed in popular culture as rock-solid, wealth-creating, safe havens where you and your loved ones can find refuge from the unrelenting storm that is the scary, presumably zombie-infested, inferior, non-house-having outside world.

Piffle. Nothing could be further from the truth.

Back in the real world, houses are saggy, expensive, leaky, high-maintenance evidence of the inevitable triumph of entropy over mankind's creations. Houses embody the vagaries of our tenuous relationship with earth and nature, and the dubious wisdom of boxing up unrelated strangers and their flammable belongings in close proximity to one another. Houses bite.

A house is a cruel master, demanding more money than can ever be provided. There's nothing—nothing—in a house or on its grounds that doesn't require a never-ending flood of cash. Every dollar selfishly squandered on food or recreation or any other non-house purpose will cost dearly over the long haul. For houses are evil and will punish for such negligence.

Thinking of buying dinner, or gas, instead of caulk for that bedroom window? Fool! The lack of caulk will spawn a leak ruining not only the window and the carpet, but allowing fetid water to cultivate a crop of black mold inside the wall that ultimately will render the entire house inhabitable. No. Your insurance won't cover that.

Each day will bring a new malfunctioning appliance, a closet door fallen from its track onto a bare foot, or a potentially deadly new leak or rattle or smell. Each repair will spawn a dozen other even more serious problems.

Each repair also opens an infinite regress. Each will haunt forever with doubts and worry. In the middle of the night a house owner will awaken and realize it's raining outside, wondering: is that sump pump really fixed? Doubts will gnaw. Didn't that repairman seem a bit shifty? Didn't he use an awful lot of duct tape? Wasn't it strange how he demanded to be paid in cash, wiped his fingerprints off everything, and fled on foot without giving a receipt?

Rain pounds on the roof and rivulets of water seep down through a million cracks and faults in the topsoil.

Is the basement now silently filling with icy floodwaters that will short out the breaker box, destroy the new washer and dryer and boxes of family treasures, and plunge the family into bankruptcy and despair? Only a panicked, chilly, shin-barking 3am trip to the cellar will allay such fears. Until the next rainstorm, when the doubts will return. Sleep well.

> My favorite neighbor: *"This guy mows his yard at 3:00 am with an industrial type light jerry rigged on top of his lawn mower which is being powered by a generator which is in turn being illuminated by his car headlights as he's always having to tinker with it. This is in a typical suburban neighborhood mind you. This guy wears those long rain boots and yellow rubber gloves while he's going at it. It looks like the godd*mn apocalypse."*

Real Estate Agents®©™

One of the most critical cogs in the house-pushing machine is your local real estate sales agent. These are the seemingly innocuous folks who put signs in yards, unlock doors, tell you where to sign the papers and arrange for you to hire their brother-in-law the home inspector. Seems helpful and kind of nice, right?

Appearances can be deceiving. The National Association of Realtors® is one of the largest, most powerful, and richest lobbying groups in the US. In one recent four year period the NAR spent $99,000,000 (ninety-nine-million dollars) just on lobbying. This sum doesn't include advertising or other propaganda. Just lobbying. Absolutely nothing of consequence happens in the world of houses, zoning, finance, building codes or related regulations that doesn't have the NAR's fingerprints on it. They all-but write the laws that "regulate" them.

Political watchdogs rate real estate industry money as among the most powerful influences on all state politics and, in about one-third of states, it's the single most powerful influence (this group includes developers and builders as well as real estate brokers.)

Did you notice the cute little ® symbol next to the word "Realtor®?" The NAR is known to be amazingly litigious and has registered the title "Realtors®" with the US Trademark office. Technically, this means that no one can use the title "Realtor®" without noting that it's a registered trademark. Like this:®. The NAR safeguards this and other logos and marks and phrases as part of their dedication to the insufferably pretentious proposition that these house-for-sale door openers are a "profession." Like

> Fun fact: A recent study by the National Bureau of Economic Research found that a doubling of the rate of house ownership in a U.S. state is later followed by a more than doubling of the rate of unemployment.

doctors and lawyers and engineers and people with actual education and skills. In lieu of an egg-headed, ivory-tower Ph.D. or M.B.A., however, those preparing to take the rigorous one-Saturday-afternoon real estate licensing quiz might be required to complete as many as *three* college level classes.[6]

Hypothetically, if we were to joke that "Realtors®" are the house-pushing equivalent of pimps, skimming money from their prostitutes while jacking up prices for johns, paying off the cops, and making an already sordid business that much sleazier, the NAR might get lawyered up and serve us papers. So we'd never write or say anything like that. And if we did, which we wouldn't, we'd be kidding. Because parody and satire. This is a funny book.

Don't make me slap you... with extra fees.

Nonetheless, the question arises: where did the sign-planters® manage to get $99,000,000 to sprinkle on elected officials? Might one safely assume that selling and reselling real estate is a lucrative business?

Let's look at a simplified example, just to give you a taste of how this works. The average real estate agent will collect 6% to 7% of a seller's profit. In this case, if you were to sell a $200,000 house, that commission equals $12,000 to $14,000.

If you had lived in such a $200,000 house for five years, paid astounding amounts in interest, taxes, PMI, repairs, maintenance, house insurance and other costs and fees and expenses, and then for some reason you sell the house, it's almost certain _the real estate agency will get more money from the sale than you will_.

Someone has to pay for your Congressman's trip to the NAR® convention in Bermuda and the lawsuits against people using the word Realtor.®

Value of $200,000 house after five years	$220,816
Rent saved	$ 78,000
Still owe on house	-$171,147
Cash out of pocket so far	-$124,246
Opportunity cost (investment)	-$ 30,483
Real estate fee of 6.5%	-$ 14,353
Your loss (so far)	-$ 41,413

---

6 If your Realtor® lets slip that he or she has a "Master's Degree," know that "REALTOR® University (NAR's for-profit, on line school) offers these made-to-order Masters' Degrees. Seriously. So far though, no football team. If you decide, mid-book, to pursue such a degree keep this caveat in mind: "REALTOR® University does not meet the requirements and approvals for licensure education; however, the education provided does complement licensure courses for a licensed real estate practitioner in many states. REALTOR® University academic programs do not prepare for or lead to licensure or meet state-specific licensure requirements."

Introduction

I'll take two Congressmen and that Senator.

Let's see. The good news is that in this example your house has increased in value! They don't always. The bad news is… Oh. Wow. Well, today you're losing $41,413. Your real estate friend® is making $14,353.

Now we know why *you* can't afford to lobby Congress. Loser.

In addition to collecting 6% or 7% of the value of each house every time it changes hands,[7] real estate agents spend their days talking to people just like you. They know your fears and concerns. They have readied glib and content-free answers. They go to seminars to learn how to "get past the no."

- "I know you said you didn't want a corner lot, but all of the properties I have listed have corners. They're all squares and rectangles. One of the realities of home shopping is that we have to make compromises."

- "I think that species of tree doesn't have leaves or bark. Our tree consultant says it's rare and expensive and supposed to look like that."

- "You have llamas? Well, as far as I know there are no specific anti-llama ordinances in this neighborhood. And the third bedroom has a sliding door for easy access."

As an added bonus every day real estate agents refer potential house buyers to surveyors and home inspectors and pest control companies. Every day. They build up mutually dependent relationships. So if one of these services providers were to feel conflicted, maybe, about whether some cost or finding or issue might harm the interests of their buddy the real estate agent (whom they work with every day) or might result in great cost or inconvenience to you (a random house buyer whom they will likely never see again) one must stop and ponder where their loyalty might lie. Hmmmm. (Hint: you're not likely be the top priority.)

Fear not! Realtors® are highly trained experts whose vast expertise and knowledge of the ins and outs of house buying could save you tens of thousands of dollars and years of unhappiness.

Or so they claim in their lobbying literature.

---

7 If you think that's steep, realize that commercial real estate brokers often make 10%

A Real Life Real Estate Anecdote

A few years back your author was interested in a house in a middle-class neighborhood in a college town in the Midwest. So interested, in fact, that I was getting ready to make an offer.

The real estate agent, who may or may not have been a Realtor® (I don't recall noticing the ® hovering over her head) was meeting me at the house with all the house info available. Let's call her "Gail®[8]" and give her a ® just to be safe.

While waiting for Gail® to take a call I noticed something interesting on the survey plat map in the paperwork. There were no details of the utility right of way in the back yard. The utility wires hung right over the center of the back yard and patio so this issue was of some concern. I was hoping I'd find an easy answer to my right-of-way question. Instead, I found something very, very odd.

"Gail®, about the back yard. While you were on the phone I was looking at this plat map again."

"I called the office about that last week," Gail® said. "They told me it's very common to have a utility right of way through a yard like this in town." She® smiled a condescending little smile.

"Fine. But this isn't a right of way. It looks like the back yard is a separate parcel. See how the property line runs right along the back of the house and the dimensions of the property only reach to this line? It looks like the property ends here at the back of the house. The lines are even a different color."

"That isn't possible," Gail® said, as if that was the end of the matter.

"Well, I'm going to need to have this resolved before we go any further," I told Gail.® "This is very strange."

To her credit Gail® did not roll her eyes at me. That must be one of the skills Realtors® learn at seminars they attend with Congressmen in Bermuda. "What would you like me to do?" she® asked. "I really don't think there's a problem so I don't know how we can resolve it."

"Do you have an attorney in your office, or a surveyor, or someone with experience in property law…?" I wasn't looking at Gail® I was looking at the property line on the survey map. So I might have missed her® head spinning around and her® eyes shooting lasers at me.

"*I* have experience with real estate," Gail® said coldly through closed teeth. "And I think you're worried over nothing." ("You arrogant and annoying asshole," she® didn't add.)

My favorite neighbor: *"If it's above 60 degrees my neighbor refuses to wear anything else but booty shorts and boots. He's a 60 year old retiree. Since he is retired he has lots of time to mow the lawn, wash his cars, BBQ, do some amateur astronomy, and work out outside in his preferred wardrobe."*

---

[8] Because that was her® name

A Real Life Real Estate Anecdote

"Can we call your office? Please? Or maybe I could take this stuff with me? I'd like to see if we can figure this out."

I wandered out the back door with my papers and Gail*, in lieu of strangling me, called her* office. I was poking around under some shrubs when she* came out of the back door and asked me if I'd like to talk to whoever was on her* phone.

The office real estate attorney or surveyor or whatever he was (he never told me his title or his name) was a bit more receptive. It only took him a few minutes to check a copy of the plat map and to agree that something was odd. "That's not a right of way," he said. "It looks like the back yard is a separate parcel. See how the property line runs right along the back of the house and the dimensions of the property only reach to this line."

"And I found a flagged survey stake in the shrubs at the edge of the patio," I told him.

"Really? A flagged survey stake?" My nameless friend paused. "Can you give me till tomorrow to try to figure out what's going on?"

The next morning the man from Gail's* office called back. "So, technically the back yard is a separate property."

"Technically?"

"Yeah, legally. But the utility has provided an easement for the property owner to use it for a back yard," he explained.

> "Home Inspectors? We had an inspector go over our house before we bought it and note there was no attic or crawl space. I toured the house with my girlfriend and we immediately saw access to it from the landing. Got a ladder and viola, found all sorts of dusty treasures. I wonder what else we paid him to miss?"

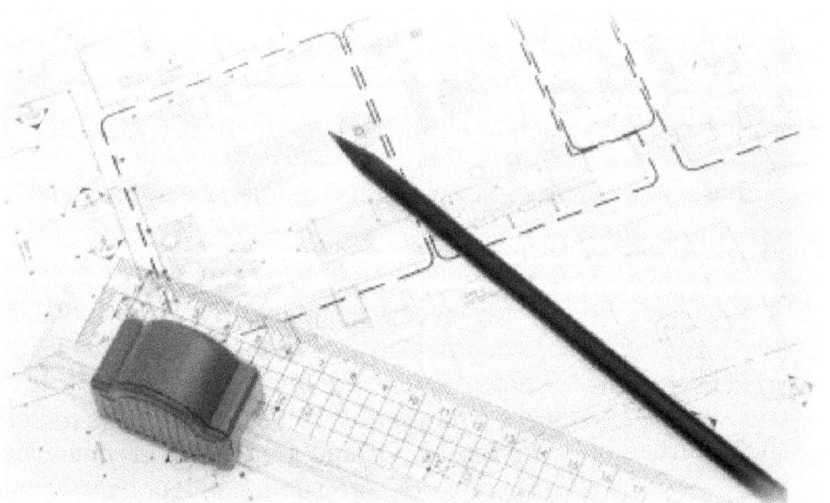

So this bedroom belongs to someone in Canada? Will that hurt resale?

"To *use* as a back yard? The house doesn't actually *have* a back yard?"

"Technically. But the situation has apparently worked for years. What happened is that the utility company bought the house, divided the property, kept the back yard and then sold the house. But they gave the house owner an easement to use the yard. So everything is okay."

18   Open House: Debunking the Myth of the "Happy Homeowner"

> **My favorite neighbor:** *"There's a man in my parents' neighborhood who sold the ~$400,000 home he built because of a dispute about a street lamp with neighbors. He then moved about a half mile up the street and built another ~$400,000 home. It has no landscaping, no sidewalk, no front steps and every Halloween he parallel parks his car at the end of his driveway. Back in high school we used to walk around the car and knock on his door anyway. Surprisingly he would still answer and get us candy even if he seemed grumpy about it all."*

"So if I buy this house, I don't own the yard? Or the patio? Or the sidewalk? Fence, trees, shrubs? Nothing?"

"Right. I guess. Technically it isn't part of the property."

"And you aren't telling people? Gail® doesn't even know this so she® isn't telling people. Is that even legal? Can you sell a house with no yard?[9]" I was standing in my kitchen staring at my phone as if it had grown tentacles.

"Well. I'm telling you. Most people don't ask. Technically it's a separate parcel, but at the end of the day it doesn't matter."

"But...there isn't even enough land to walk to the back door," I protested. "How can that not matter? The second I step outside I'm on someone else's property. The driveway runs across that land. So it's landlocked except for the front walk. What if they decide to revoke the easement?'

"Oh, they wouldn't do that."

I didn't buy that house from Gail®. But I did learn a lot. Someone else bought the house and Gail® and her office made their $14,500. I suspect the new buyers never asked about the back yard or its technical nonexistence. Why would they?

Imagine their surprise, one day, when they apply for a building permit to add a gazebo or kid's playhouse or wake up one day to a fence across their driveway and back door.

Not to worry. You still have an easement. It's just lower now.

---

9 I was so naive back then. Of course it's legal.

> *"Whenever you find yourself on the side of the majority it is time to pause and reflect."*   Mark Twain

The "Starter House"

Financial experts agree: before you consider financing a house you should save up at least a 20% down payment, plus an emergency fund, build up excellent credit to get the best terms, and make certain you'll stay in the house for as long as possible—preferably the entire term of the mortgage.

Hey. Wait a minute. Given how few Americans prioritize that sort of fiscal responsibility, wouldn't waiting and saving and doing all of that other stuff cut into Gail's® lobbying money?

Indeed it would.

So naturally some smart cookie (in the house-pushing industry?) created the idea of buying a "starter house" to live in while…while…what? How does that work?

- If you buy a "starter house," (a cheap house you really don't want) how can you be saving for a more expensive house that you really do want?
- If your only chance to make money on a house is by staying put long term, how can it make financial sense to buy a house you intend to sell in a few years?
- If transaction costs eat up so much of a house's profit, how can doubling the transaction costs by buying and selling an additional houses make sense?
- It *doesn't* make sense if you stop and think about it. Which people apparently don't.

Maybe throwing money down the small pit of a starter house is supposed to be practice for throwing even more money down a deeper pit with a bigger more expensive house? Sounds like a grand idea.

As we'll spend many pages examining in detail, financing a house is ~~usually~~ always a money-losing project. Your only hope of even breaking-even[10] on a standard house financing deal is to stay put, be frugal, and pay off the mortgage without incurring any more transaction costs; costs like financing and insuring and maintaining and updating and selling a starter house.

> My favorite neighbor: *"I'm a cop. I once responded to a domestic disturbance to find two neighbors blowing leaves at each other with little portable leaf blowers. They were serious. Angry and everything."*

---

10 Actually, you *can't* break even with conventional financing in most situations. Not even close. But hope springs eternal.

Think of a "starter house" as a big, expensive, wooden, oxymoronic symbol, representing everything stupid, costly and disingenuous about the entire house financing industry. Like a "savings account" you pay for, a "sale" with higher prices, or "clear skies" legislation that encourages pollution.

We haven't been able to definitively trace the origin of the pernicious concept of the "starter house" so we've decided to blame it on the real estate people because they're the most obvious beneficiaries.

Our friend Gail® and her fellow legislative-junket-underwriters make money on transition costs. Each time a house is bought or sold they get paid. If you, the buyer or seller, make money, lose money …it doesn't matter. Even if you lose the house, guess who makes money?

Short sales. Foreclosures. There they® are, like a toll booth on the great turnpike of real estate transactions, making money from each transfer that goes by. So if you buy, and sell, an extra house guess who® gets paid?

I used to sell houses, but I just couldn't look myself in the mirror, ya know?

If the NAR® didn't actually create the idea of the "starter house" they certainly have profited from it and done little to discourage the concept. You'd hope an "agent®" with an apparent fiduciary duty[11] to look out for your best interest would discourage you from making such a bad decision.

Wouldn't it be nice if that were the case?

The House Financing Industry

Enabling America's addiction to financing a never-ending series of ever-larger, money-wasting houses is a solemn duty. Also a very lucrative one.

Stepping up to ~~take all this money~~ volunteer for this duty are the brave women and men (but mostly men) of the house financing industry.

From the small fry paper-signers and sales pros at your local credit union all the way up to the so-sharp-

---

11 We say "apparent" because in reality the real estate person trying to sell you a house isn't acting for your benefit any more than the car salesman at "Big Al's House of Wrecks" is acting on your behalf. Such relationships vary by state, and by individual circumstances, but are always complicated and difficult to figure out for a consumer. General rule: Real state brokerages are not "your agent," not like having an attorney representing your interests, and generally real estate folks are *not* looking out exclusively for your interests. *Caveat emptor.*

The House Financing Industry

as-to-be-sociopathic big brokerage houses on Wall Street, these are the savviest financial minds on the planet. These are the people who have made a science out of "the most house you can afford," ensuring America's economy will get maximum benefit from all the debt you can possibly take on. And more!

These are the people who created debt-based financial instruments so complex and bizarre they themselves could not understand or properly monitor them; worthless financial instruments worth three times the value of the entire world economy! These are the people who then, collectively, threw up their hands and pled innocence when this vast market in imaginary abstractions popped like a dollar store balloon and almost sent the entire world economy into a death spiral back in 2008.

Indeed, when almost every one of the 65% of Americans (65% at that time) who owned a house at that time lost tens or hundreds of thousands of dollars overnight, these house financers are the people who hid under their desks, pointed fingers at one another, and finally decided the real guilty party was poor people who had outsmarted them by somehow qualifying for house loans they couldn't afford. (Really. That's what they said.)

These are the very same people who will make from 60% to 120% of the value of a house from the financing, even if the buyer loses their shirt and other critical garments, even if they lose the house itself. These are the people who get paid first.

By now we hope your shield of cynicism is strong and you aren't shocked to learn that these self-same house financers are among the most ardent supporters of promiscuous house buying.

Yes! These are the people who want you to finance a house and to rely upon their advice when doing so.

Sounds like a great idea, right?

Even during the darkest days of the 2008 housing collapse, when it looked like we all might be approaching our credit unions to inquire about cave dwellings, these brave heroes of the house financing industry never gave up.

"The time to buy is now!" was their battle cry.

If the market is high? "Value is maximized!" Market is low? "Opportunity knocks!" Market falling like a drunken celebrity down the stairs at a music awards show? "Historic opportunity!!"

According to these experts with their fingers on the pulse of the house market, there's never a bad time to buy.

For example: "There's never a bad time to buy," is an actual quote from one of their media-saturating propaganda campaigns.

To anyone paying attention, this obsessive insistence that there's "never a bad time" to buy a house might tend to undermine the argument that house buying is a sane and rational act. After all, in other areas of life we assume there are times to step up, and times to step away.

Revelry for example. Certainly a good thing. Let the fun begin! But let's skip the big post-game riot with the flaming and overturned police cars, shall we?

If the house financing industry were promoting parties, they would likely urge us to grab some gasoline and rags because, "Hey! There's never a bad time to riot!" Even the multi-trillion dollar hangover from 2008's housing collapse hasn't changed their minds. Maybe that's because they're partying with our money?

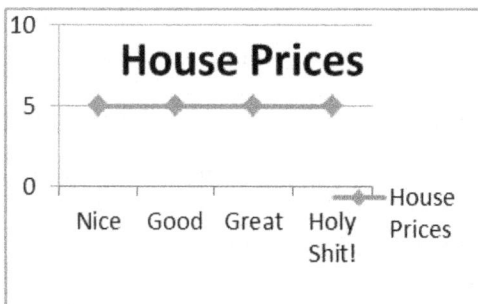

The signs! They are perfect! You must buy now!

Sadly, none of this has changed *our* minds either. Recent surveys by Fannie Mae and the Demand Institute show that the vast majority of Millennials still buy into the House Myth and look forward to financing a house of their own. Let's say that again. Even the kids who came of age just as their parents were forced to sell off younger siblings to bail out their overvalued, underwater houses still want one of their own! (A house, not another sibling.)

Lucky for the house financers, few Americans are paying attention. Such is the Power of Myth.

The House Financing Industry

These days, post collapse, post hangover, post forehead-palming, post blame-the-house-buyers, what do our friends® in the house pushing industry tell us about buying a house?

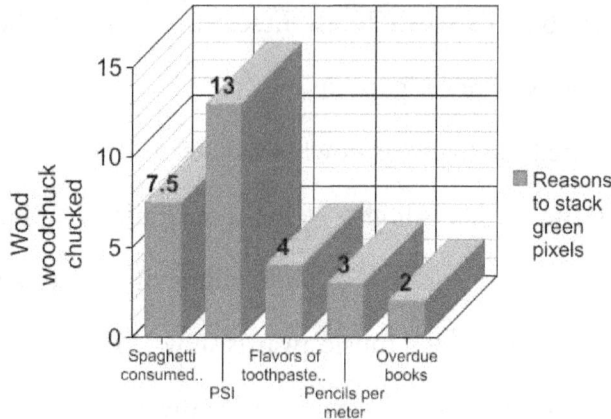

Typical house-pusher "information"

Let's say, for a moment, that you're a high school graduate without a college diploma or have a trade degree. Maybe you make about eighteen dollars per hour. You could be a Court Reporter or a Delivery Driver or even an EMT. Your annual wages at eighteen dollars on hour are about $36,000 per year. Our experts suggest: Finance a house!

Our advice[12] is that you can't afford to finance a house and probably shouldn't even be wasting cash on ridiculous books like this. If you only make $36,000 a year and have four kids, for example, you could qualify for public assistance (according to the U.S. government). With only three kids if you live in Alaska or Hawaii. But our allegedly newly cautious, post-collapse friends in the house financing industry want you to buy a house on the way to pick up that welfare check.

Sound strange to you? Let's dig deeper.

According to the people® with $99,000,000 to throw around for lobbying if you make $36,000 a year you "can afford" a house that costs…Holy crap…$165,000?!?

Are you serious, "Realtor.com?®"

This is their self-described "conservative" calculation, by the way. Apparently their greedy recklessness has a "moderate" and an "aggressive" setting as well. (It goes all the way up to 11, Nigel![13])

Do you want to end up in bankruptcy court? Because that is how you end up in bankruptcy court. Or selling plasma to make ends meet. Or shooting up on dirty mattresses

---

12 Ha. Fooled you. We told you nothing in this goofy book is advice. Are you not paying attention?

13 Our editor feared some wouldn't get this reference. If so we are really disappointed.

behind boarded-up storefronts.

If we were serious people writing a serious book (which we're not) and we were offering advice (which we're not) we'd consider telling you to ignore that kind of "information" from people who stand to make hundreds of thousands of dollars merely by having you sign some papers.

Please consider ignoring the sales pitches of people who want to ruin your life so they can afford to spend nine figures a year making laws designed to help them make even more money.

Laugh in the face of someone who tells you that taking on ruinous debt could—under impossible conditions—result in your "making money" even though a quick look at the facts says otherwise.

Examine the largest purchase most people ever make with the same critical eye you'd use to shop for a Groupon® or compare deals on a vacuum cleaner.

Your Best Friend, the House Expert

House buying: what a cluster! So confusing. What is real? What is illusion? What is tru...uuu...uuth?[14] What to do?

Luckily, you're surrounded by a bevy of self-appointed experts eager to guide you through this labyrinth of house shopping, financing, upkeep and, if you heed their advice, eventual financial ruin and calls to the suicide prevention hotline. They're your friends and family. They know everything!

As with the subjects of child rearing and driving, each person on the face of the earth seems to think they're an expert on houses. All of them are just trembling with eagerness to contradict you, argue with you, and instruct you to do really stupid things.

As we researched this book on houses (which is more effort than your local "experts" will ever put into the subject) and were very obviously educating and informing ourselves in plain view from a font of well-regarded and verifiable sources, nonetheless, nearly every human being who found out about the project stepped up

---

14 Another brilliant but subtle comedic reference our Editor thought might befuddle some of you. "Existential Blues" by Tom "T-Bone" Stankus. Make certain your version has the banned "dream the impossible dream" lyric.

and offered horrible, unsolicited advice.

- "Homes are a great investment," said a cousin who, along with her husband, owns two underwater houses.
- "Everyone needs to own a house," said my mother, who lives in a subsidized rental and has never even held a job or a drivers' license.
- "You can always count on real estate to appreciate," said the neighbors who lost $120,000 in equity during the 2008 crash and then turned right around and took out a second mortgage this year.
- "Owning a house gives you stability," offered a former neighbor who walked away from her house and allowed it to be foreclosed.
- "You'd have to be a fool to pay rent when you could invest your money in a house," said a high school buddy who owns nothing and lives with his girlfriend.

All of these people, none of whom have any credentials in real estate or financing or law, none of whom have made one single nickel in real estate, all took time out of their busy days to offer horrible advice.

You have people just like this in your life. Wonderful people, people whom you love, people who love you and want to help.

Smile and nod if you can, let them know you appreciate their concern, but for goodness sakes ignore them.

House of Cards

Like failed middle-school science experiments, houses begin to fall apart even before they're finished.

Foundations sink and settle. Concrete cracks. Walls shift. Wood warps and separates. The resulting stresses open more leaks for water and insects and weather and that causes more damage. Serious damage. Deep-seated, expensive, unseen damage. Drywall becomes damp; mold grows. Wood rots. Floors sag. Pipes leak, wires fray, and pests invade. Solid parts loosen up and moving parts stop. Drains stop draining; pumps stop pumping.

Meanwhile, outside, flimsy shingles and trim loosen in the wind and blow into the neighbor's yard, causing festering resentment as well as expensive cosmetic damage. Dogs pee on the mailbox, rotting the post.

> "Our house, being a house, is constantly trying to degenerate into a random pile of hardware so we are constantly trying to get people to come fix things."
> --Dave Barry

House remodelers and builders can be masters at concealing such ubiquitous defects. Real estate agents are their willing accomplices. Home inspectors add a sheen of polish by officially missing things. Working together they cover up the worst and most expensive horrors and make other problems sound like luxury options.

Politicians and ad men are rank amateurs at weasel words compared to those in the house-pushing industry, who might explain with a smile why it's perfectly normal to have hot water only on odd-numbered days: 'Think of the energy savings!' they® might say.

Perversely, once you're conned into financing a house, you'll learn to relish the process of uncovering the flaws and mistakes that have been painted over by these hucksters. Your house scab-picking will inevitably become a masochistic new hobby. You'll seek, and find, adventure behind every panel:

> *"Sweet Jesus, Abby, willya look at this mess of wires taped together up in this ceiling?? It's a damned electrified knot of half-melted plastic. And it's almost touching this gas pipe. I'm gonna see if I can push it over to one side…. Here. Hold my beer."*

Such masochistic fault-finding is mandatory. It's public. It's the house owner equivalent of releasing a sex tape.[15]

House owners are required to share these miserable revelations with their neighbors as you all struggle to find common ground among this tribe of intimately abutting strangers who now inhabit each other's lives.

However, also like releasing a sex tape, know that sharing house horror stories with neighbors is a desperate cry for help.

You and your fellow house owners will congregate awkwardly together

I don't remember the real estate agent showing us this bathroom.

---

15 Wisely we decided not to illustrate this point with an image.

House of Cards

—often in the street or on someone's cracked and sunken driveway—and compete in a game of outrage and frustration. Which faulty wiring is more likely to cause a fatal home fire? Who owes more money to her plumber? And (everyone look down at that concrete) whose sunken driveway has cost more to shore up so far?

> My favorite neighbor: *"My neighbor has OCD for sure. He mows and leaf blows his yard every day. Every single day. If it rains, the second it stops he goes out there to mow and leaf blow. He leaf blows his roof. Then he leaf blows his cars. Then washes his cars. Every day. He either has OCD or hates his wife. He never talks or waves to anyone either. Strange dude. The neighborhood kids super glued a leaf to his driveway one time. I wish I had been there to see his reaction."*

This pathetic activity is what passes for bonding and socialization among the house owning class. This is what you'll be reduced to.

Enjoy such meager social pleasure while you can. Soon you'll have to abandon the others to run back home and finish cleaning the gutters, again, before the big rain forecast for the weekend.

That reminds us.... How is your sump pump working?

To really understand the nature of a new life as a house owner, think of a house like a sandcastle as high tide approaches. You're the small child with a bucket and shovel fighting a losing battle with the vast sea. Crying is a waste of time. Giving up and letting go is your only option.

Accept the loss of what you value and hold dear. Nothing lasts.

Like sands through the hourglass, your house is dust in the wind on a stairway to heaven.

Chapter 1 take-aways:
- Only a long prison sentence or the sort of accident that leads to amputation and a respirator can do more to ruin your life than financing a house.
- House-pushers have spent decades and hundreds of millions of dollars creating the false myth of the "Happy Homeowner."
- Real estate salespeople make a lot of money convincing families to spend too much on houses they know little about.
- So called "starter houses" are one of the worst purchases a family can make, and one of the best examples of how hypocritical and ridiculous house-pushing propaganda can be.
- The house pushing industries learned nothing from 2008 and will, if you allow them, sign you up for the sort of crippling debt that causes divorces and suicides.
- The house financing industry makes billions of dollars a year selling overpriced houses at usurious interest rates, and by adding layers of hidden but debilitatingly expensive costs to people (like you and me) who have no idea what they are getting into.
- Most people have been buffaloed by the myths, lies and BS of the house pushers and, if asked, despite not having a clue, will parrot back to you the most ridiculous of the house owning myths. Ignore them.
- Modern American houses are shoddily constructed, poorly designed, fragile collections of junk and medieval technology purposely built as cheaply as possible with the intention of becoming obsolete, and will cost you a significant portion of your income just to prevent them from falling in on your head.

Keep wishing!
Its almost gone!

Chapter 2: No Money for You!

Almost no one "makes money" from merely financing and owning a house. It's like going to Vegas: the house wins!

The house-selling industry has performed an amazing feat of prestidigitation by convincing most people that simply living in a house and paying the bills will result, over time, in a life-changing windfall of magical money. This trick was accomplished using three general strategies:

First, the house pushers vastly underestimate the costs of owning a house. Second, they vastly overestimate the profits to be made. Third, they overhype the other benefits of owning a house and minimize the nightmares, turning these mythical benefits into "extra value" allegedly weighing in favor of house buying.

"Wow! If you buy a house you could run a small factory[16] or raise llamas in your spare bedroom[17] and it's all tax free![18]"

Let's take that path way down there. It looks more...um... well-traveled.

Our Example House

House costs vary widely depending upon where you live—city, country, suburbs. In some ritzy neighborhoods it's possible to easily spend eight or nine figures for a house if you can afford to do so. Thanks to Gail® and her friends in the finance industry, you could end up spending that much even if you *can't* afford to do so.

On the other hand, if you look in seedy rural areas or blighted urban zones, a livable house is available for as little as $30,000.

People shopping those extremes probably aren't buying books like this about houses. So we'll assume you're interested in a more typical, middle-class house.

---

16 No, you can't.

17 No, you can't.

18 No, it isn't.

The mean price of a new house in the United States in the summer of 2015 was $272,900. The median price was a bit less: $221,800. Huge, high-priced houses skew the new house numbers toward the larger end. Few are building 900 square foot houses these days.[19]

Houses overall (new and pre-soiled) average about $170,000 with a skew towards the older, smaller house stock in urban and depressed rural areas.

> My favorite neighbor: *"He is a hoarder and at night when the lights are on inside the house you can see the stacks of stuff piled to the ceiling so that almost no light escapes the window. He must have made a mess of the kitchen because he keeps his groceries in the trunk of his Hyundai and eats out of it. In the summer he'll sit on his front steps with his trunk open and eat sandwiches with the birds eating extra bread next to him."*

With all of these numbers in mind, we're going to do our figuring based on a house that sells for a nice, middle-of-the-road $200,000.

Our $200,000 price tag isn't just lower than the average new house price, which means we have to work harder to prove the house-pushers wrong, it's an easy figure to work with. That Nebraska or Alabama farmhouse selling for $50,000? That's exactly 25% of our example. Adjust accordingly. The pricier house selling for $400,000? Just double our numbers.

For this scenario we'll be assuming that you, our hypothetical buyer, have better than average credit, are putting $10,000 down, are getting a pretty decent 4% fixed rate loan over 30 years, and are not shackling yourself to a Home Owners Association. All of these assumptions skew toward lowering your costs and helping the pro-house people prove their point. Many people in real buying situations will see much higher costs. We are ignoring inflation both in our costs and our values. They rise or fall together and balance out in the end.

What Counts as House Owning Costs?

If you're waiting to buy a house before you adopt a Mastiff or to start raising goats, do the animal-related expenses count as costs of owning a house? We don't count those kinds of expenses in our figures, but you will need to budget for them.

Some people buy a house and start collecting art, or junk, or both. If they didn't own a house, would they spend $100,000 over 30 years collecting autographed athletic cups and framed metal gas station signs from

---

19 Our editor said we should acknowledge the "Tiny House" phenom. Thus far tiny houses are about as popular as commuting to work on electric scooters but, hey, they make for cool news stories and cute photos, don't they? Acknowledged.

the Depression? Does this mean that hoarding becomes one cost of owning a house? Hard to give a definitive answer. But, for the purposes of this book, we'll say no.

Many people wait to have kids until they buy a house. Two of life's most expensive and time-consuming projects embarked upon together.

Again, we don't count these things as a cost of owning a house.

As a potential house owner, however, maybe you've created an emotional connection between buying a house and quilting, or raising ferrets. Maybe, for you, buying a house is a prerequisite for bringing home those four foster kids, or building a glass-blowing furnace in the back yard?

In that case maybe you should include those costs in your new house owning budget. But we'll leave that math up to you.

We are going to stick to the fundamentals. The nuts and bolts stuff the house pushers ignore so they can make houses sound less like financial suicide.

Most of the *real* costs of owning a house don't appear in the helpful guides from real estate agents or the credit union. They're not included in the "budget for a house" worksheets that are supposed to convince us all houses are great investments.

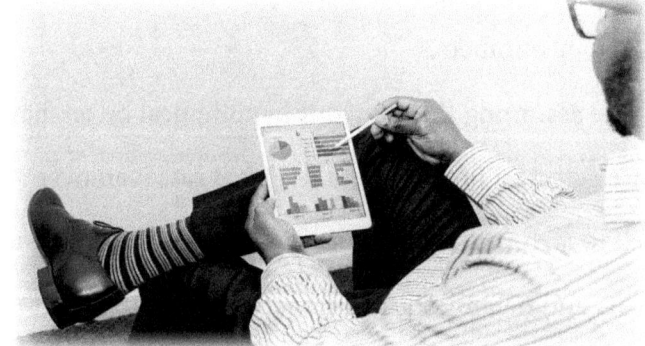

If you keep accounting for all the money you spend on your house I won't be able to prove it makes money!

As an example, let's say you're filled with blind rage at a book (that shall remain nameless) so you run out to buy a $200,000 house just for spite. During your first year of owning said house let's say you spend $4,000 repairing, maintaining or replacing various things: paint, filters, leaks. Add in a furnace "tune up" and some landscaping, maybe the cost of hiring a licensed plumber to finally come out and take care of that sump pump. Plus one new major appliance. Maybe get rid of that weird little steam powered dish washer in the back yard and replace it with an electric model in the kitchen.

Does this $4,000 you've now spent on the house count as a cost of owning that house? Do you figure in this $4,000 when deciding if owning the house is cheaper than rent, is saving money and is a "smart investment?"

What Counts as House Owning Costs

What foolish and simple-minded questions you ask!

You see, according to the house pushers, repairing or replacing or maintaining or upgrading everything about your house, not just your mechanicals and appliances, should only cost about 1% of the price of the house each year. In this example that would be $2000.

> *A recent study by online house-pushers Zillow and Thumbtack estimated an average house owner would spent about $9,500 per year in "hidden costs" for repair and maintenance and insurance and taxes. "...new buyers can get excited about having a backyard of their own for the first time," says Zillow, "without budgeting for how they plan to maintain that space"*

So if you spent more than $2000 in total on your house in a year, well, that's your fault! Don't be pointing your greasy fingers at the house and trying to blame it. Don't even think about going back to that real estate agent and saying, *"Hey! What the ever-loving hell? This big cardboard box of caulk and crabgrass is costing me a fortune!"*

Don't bother to post a comment on the "Happy Homebuyers' Guide" website noting that their advice sucked.

In order to fall in line with the Happy House-owner Myth, you aren't supposed to count what you actually *spend* on a house as a house ownership cost. You can only count what the house pushers tell you to count. Otherwise their sparkly, happy math doesn't work.

What if, for another example, like many new house buyers, you decide to make a bunch of additional changes and upgrades after you purchase your home. Let's say you spend an extra $2,600 (on top of that previous $4,000) on gutter repair, new, non-smoldering wiring for the garage, and to tear up and replace the musty shag carpet in the rumpus room.

Even though your real estate agent may have encouraged these costly changes when you looked at the house ("Don't let the smoke rolling out of the electric sockets or the paisley carpet stop you. Imagine what it will look like after you've made it your own!"), according to the terms of the house-pusher's math, you've really screwed up.

Now that you've pissed away $6,600 in repairs and maintenance, you've spent more than triple what you were supposed to spend in a year.

Wow. You're like a drunken sailor on shore leave, aren't you?

Or like a real estate sales agent who just resold the same house for the third time.

What Counts as House Owning Costs

Does this mean the house pusher math was wrong? No! Does it mean their estimates were too low? No! Could it be that they're trying to drastically downplay the real cost of owning a house? Of course not! What are we here, some kind of crazy conspiracy theorists in tinfoil hats? Get outta here with those Oliver Stone conspiracies.[20] Of course that isn't what happened.

Apologists from the house owning lobby will quibble with such examples. "Quibble" being a polite understatement. The house pushers will insist that some or all of those costs either "don't count" as costs of house owning at all, or should be placed in another accounting column, or should be covered by insurance, and, if they're not covered, you should have bought better insurance, or should have dealt preemptively with the issue through earlier maintenance, or the problem should have been uncovered during a home inspection, and if it wasn't, you should have paid for a better home inspection…etc., etc., etc.

I'd call a plumber but I've already spent 1.7% of the house's value this year!!

Whew! I guess they expect us to go back and review each and every house expense. Using their rules. And their categories. And their accounting. They know a *priori*[21] that such expenses don't count because they made up the definitions and they say such things don't count.

Notice a commonality among all the objections in the mouth of our apologist for the house-pushing racket? Each and every one of them is just a fancy way of stating: "It's your fault!"

It's *Your* Fault!

You should have kept up on the maintenance before you even bought the house. You should have been able to predict the specific failures and repairs before you bought the house so when the home inspection

---

20 Because jet fuel can't melt steel beams!

21 Another fancy Latin word for that term paper. It means they knew before they even started.

didn't find them you'd know to get another home inspection.[22] You should have bought other/better/additional insurance that would cover the specific problems you had yet to experience.[23]

You should have doctorate-level knowledge of all of this insurance/inspection/prediction stuff, plus the current market value of equipment, repair, and maintenance of a dozen different sorts of infrastructure covered by a dozen different sorts of skilled trades. Why don't you have several advanced degrees in running your new house-owning corporation? You failed. Your fault. Slacker.

> My favorite neighbor: *"Guy down the street from me owns a rooster. I don't even live in the country, like the street I live on is your typical suburban cul-de-sac. And this f*cking rooster wakes me up at the crack of dawn every single day during the summer. No Idea where he keeps it during the winter, but for the past three summers this has continued to happen."*

But that's not true! It *isn't* your fault. The system is rigged. This book proposes the shocking theory that maybe, just maybe, every average person stuck within this rigged system loses money by buying and financing a house the conventional way. And that's the way they want it.

To thoroughly explore and examine this revolutionary new idea we have designed a better cost/benefit algorithm designed to take into consideration the variation of housing costs from region to region and the new IRS rules for depreciation and mortgage interest as well as a scaled table for the estimated amortized cost of the money value of repair and maintenance along with the growth of equity.

Hahaha. No, no. Not really.

Instead we present a simple rule. Here is our definition of a house ownership cost: money you spend because you own a house (that you wouldn't have spent if you were merely renting).

That's it.

Financing Costs: "The Money Changers"

Most people have no idea how expensive it can be to finance and pay all the mandatory associated costs of buying a house. House pushers seem to feel that such minor issues, like the details of a prostate exam or the smells and sounds of a root canal, are best hidden until the process is already unalterably underway.

Let's take a look at these "minor figures." We'll assume you're not Bill Gates or Alice Walton and are, in-

---

[22] Yes. That would also cost more money. No. You don't get to think about that.

[23] Yes. That would also cost more money. No. You don't get to think about that.

Financing Costs: "The Money Changers"

> *"It is well enough that people of the nation do not understand our banking and monetary system, for if they did, I believe there would be a revolution before tomorrow morning."* Henry Ford

stead, just a regular old gal or guy and you had to stop at the bank and get a regular old mortgage loan to buy that $200,000 house. How does the financial deal look from the perspective of you, sitting there and writing checks?

Well, if you were lucky enough to have excellent credit and a big $40,000 down payment (the minimum for securing a loan with no expensive Private Mortgage Insurance [PMI] is 20% down, and 20% of $200,000 is $40,000) your $200,000 house with financing will actually cost about $314,932. That's just the cost of the house financing. That total doesn't include the majority of the costs: taxes, mandatory and optional insurance, repairs, upgrades, maintenance, the cost of having your money tied up for 30 years, or any of the myriad other expenses we have been discussing.

That total of $314,932 is a best-case situation, by the way. If you have to borrow money on a typical 30 year plan you're unlikely to pay less than that for financing. You're very likely to pay more.

A more realistic 30 year, $200,000 mortgage with only $10,000 down would cost $342,465 over the life of the mortgage. Ouch. Right out of the box your $200,000 house will cost you a one-third of a million dollars. Before taxes or insurance or maintenance or any other mandatory, predictable expenses. But wait. There's more. Since you only have $10,000 sitting around for a down payment you get the added joy of paying for PMI.

People who don't have a 20% down payment are required to buy PMI to ensure (and insure) the mortgage holder gets its money back. PMI helps make your mortgage "marketable" on the secondary market where such financial instruments are bought and sold. PMI isn't cheap. Why so expensive? Because someone needs to guarantee that the mortgage finance company will make its $142,465 in profit. That's what you're paying to insure: their profit on your house.

PMI isn't for your benefit. PMI is for them.

You can look at PMI as a sort of life-insurance policy on profit if we lived in the kind of world where financial institutions no longer had to take any risks in order to make obscene profits from merely moving wealth from place to place and could make even more money by charging you extra money to insure they will make those profits.

But, hey, we're already in for $342,465, right? Why quibble over a few more bucks?

The cost of this added insurance is an additional $142 per month using the numbers in our example. The good news is that you don't pay PMI forever. In most cases your lender's profit insurance is only mandatory until you pay off 20% of the principle on your mortgage. Only 20%! How long could that take?

Funny you should ask.

Because of the strange way home mortgages are structured, it's possible that you may not pay off 20% of the principle until as long as halfway through your loan period. In our charitable and optimistic example, PMI would last for eight years. (This is worth repeating: it will take at least eight years to pay off only 20% of the mortgage. And as long as fifteen years.) At this point our hypothetical house buyer will have spent at least $220,192 on the house and still owe $162,613.27

How the heck can you spend eight long years throwing $220,000 at a house that allegedly only cost $200,000 and barely have 20% of it paid off?

The answer is that most of the money you pay the bank is going to pay for interest on the loan. Not the principle. Not the $200,000 price of the house. Just the interest.

And not counting about $100,000 you paid in non-bank costs.

During the first year about 93% of your mortgage payment is toward interest, not principle. Only .07¢ of each dollar you pay goes toward the price of the house. You pay the bank its profit first. Plus the taxes. Plus the upkeep and repair and insurance and PMI. Then you get to pay for your house.

Back to the problem of PMI. To get a mortgage loan, even if you didn't have 20% of the price of the house for a down payment, you still likely paid some sort of down payment. A down payment reduces the amount you're financing for the house. If the house is priced at $200,000 and you pay $10,000 down, you only finance the remaining $190,000.

This isn't the case with PMI. The $14,100 in PMI we calculated based on our house cost and down payment is in addition to the money you are tossing at the house itself.

Unlike the down payment, this extra money doesn't reduce the amount borrowed. This $14,100 for PMI buys you nothing. Nothing except the privilege of paying ~~$342,465~~ $356,565 for a $200,000 house.

```
Mortgage:            $342,465
PMI:                 $ 14,100
$200,000 house       $356,565  (so far)
```

Next, let's take a hard look at two other fundamental costs that many people lump in (usually through a dedicated escrow account) with their monthly mortgage payment: taxes and insurance.

The Tax Man

Variations in the average cost of property taxes can make this cost seem beyond estimation: property taxes range from as low as $250 per year in rural areas of Oklahoma and Alabama to over $10,000 a year in areas of New York.

Maybe property taxes inversely track dirt roads, cornfields, or courthouse statues of Jesus riding a dinosaur? We don't know. This book doesn't explore those potentially fascinating issues.

But we do know it makes things more manageable to recognize property taxes as some percentage of a house's assessed value. And we know that the majority of house owners pay annual taxes of between 2% and 4% of the assessed value of the house.

Sounds like that would be between $4,000 and $8,000 for the $200,000 house, right? Not quite. Assessed value isn't the same thing as what a house actually sells for.

Yes, that is a bit odd.

But let's not venture too far off the main discussion highway down another side-topic-exit. For now it is enough to say that the assessed value is another example of something that was made up.

Get it? The assessed (taxable) value of a house is made up by the taxing entity; the very people who want and need the tax dollars that assessed value generates.

Back to taxes. Usually the assessed value of a house (whatever that might be) is approximately half of the selling price. So the range of 2% to 4% of a $200,000 house (assessed at $100,000) would be between $2,000 and $4,000 per year.

Using the national property tax average of 2.5% of the assessed value, ours ends up at $2,500 per year.

This means that during the course of a 30 year mortgage the house owner will pay about $75,000 ($2,500 x 30) in property taxes.

Mortgage:	$342,456
PMI:	$ 14,100
Taxes:	$ 75,000
Cost of $200,000 house:	$ 431,156

Wow. $431,156 and no one's even turned on the cable yet.

Insurance Costs

The many stakeholders in a house,[24] most especially the mortgage holder, require a house be fully insured against fire, flood, and other catastrophic happenstance. Guess who gets to pay for this mandatory insurance?

We will talk at length about insurance and insurance companies later in the book. For now, you need to know that insurance rates, like the other costs of owning a house, vary widely and wildly and seemingly without much of a pattern.

One commonality is that all mortgage holders require a certain minimum level of insurance coverage. For a $200,000 house that coverage averages between $100 and $150 per month depending upon a whole raft of variables: location, crime rate, your credit score, previous insurance claims, risk factors such as the house being in an earthquake zone or actually being on fire, the size of the house, the location of the nearest fire hydrant, "attractive nuisances" like swimming pools, even details about your family life and health.

As before, let's take a middle-of-the-road approach and estimate mandatory house insurance premium at $125 per month. ($125 x 12 months x 30 years = $45,000.)

> My favorite neighbor: My neighbor mows her lawn when it's snowing. She uses the mower to clear the driveway, then does the yard, and back to the driveway till the snow stops. She also scrapes her driveway with a shovel around 3am to make sure there is absolutely no snow on it. She has started tying bits of string between her trees, and her house, and her shrubs. We don't talk to her but my wife once asked her about the string and she screamed and tried to throw a hose and told her to mind her own business. I'm pretty sure she has been stealing our tomatoes and apples. She eats the apples and leaves the cores in our yard.

---

24 See "The Man" in Chapter 4.

Mortgage:	$342,456
PMI:	$ 14,100
Taxes	$ 75,000
Insurance	$ 45,000
Cost of $200,000 house:	$ 476,565

Replacement, Repair, and Maintenance

Standard house ownership rhetoric usually all but ignores the real, very substantial cost of repairs, maintenance, upgrades, service, replacement, and renovations including non-warrantied costs and non-insured or deductible costs.

That isn't much different or any more honest than ignoring the cost of similar work on a car. Except that even the cheapest car is a highly evolved, very dependable state-of-the-art precision machine while even the nicest house is a medieval-tech pile of toothpicks and cardboard. So, ignoring house fixin" is even worse.

Even when house upkeep costs are hinted at, the house pusher protocol is to assign them a *de minimus* number like "1% of the value of the house per year." One percent sounds like chump change, right?

Well, even that disingenuous lowball estimate of 1% of our $200,000 house equals $2,000 per year. That's the equivalent of one month's costs for mortgage, insurance, PMI and taxes. Not an insignificant amount.

Permit? This is my Bill The Builder cosplay. I thought "remodel your bathroom" was a euphemism...

The price of a flat screen and audio system, or a memorable trip to Vegas. Two thousand dollars is the sort of money you notice when it goes missing.

Note that this one variable—the cost of house upkeep—can equal the difference between making money using standard house owning calculations and losing money. So, even if you decide this book is full of cow pies and the house pushers are right, keep in mind that slight variations in the cost of keeping up your house are the difference between winning and losing this game using the house pushers' own numbers and calculations.

Change that 1% to a more realistic 2% and the mythical magical, money-producing properties of houses start malfunctioning. Bump that 1% to an honest 4% and a house will lose money even according to the most outrageous, optimistic, rose-colored, pro-house cyphering.

The sad fact is that 1% of the selling price is an ~~unrealistically~~ ridiculously low estimate of what it will cost to keep a house from falling in.

To find the true cost of keeping a house together we need, first, to ignore the house-pusher's unsupported rhetoric and look up some actual information on the cost of repairs, replacements, and preventative house care.

To that end we made accurate lists of house stuff that needs to be repaired, serviced or replaced. Then we went to the experts who make, sell, service, repair, insure, and warranty all that stuff to see what they say about costs.

Our Replacement Table lists components of your house that, at some point, will need to be replaced. Each of these components comes from the factory with an expiration date. Some are obvious: "20-year shingles,"

So-called "home warranty companies" tend to overestimate the costs and crisis level of house maintenance.

Don't gamble with the high cost of replacing major house components!

Wishing your house won't fall apart or asplode is a MAJOR GAMBLE that could cost you MILLIONS of dollars!

Quentin gambled that his doorknobs would last and LOST

Loser!!

Now he is selling plasma and working as a lot lizard.

Don't be like Quentin! Call or email or fax or text us today for your obligation-ridden high-risk evaluation that mostly consists of us confirming your credit card works!

HouseScam *a division of HomeScam, a subsidiary of Blue Sky Offshore Enterprises*

for example.

Other termination dates can be found by referring to well-known experts like Consumers' Union (the group behind <u>Consumer Reports</u>) or to insurance estimates, or to depreciation tables for value and taxes, or to the manufacturers of the item. In each case we discover that house parts and pieces are designed to last only a set length of time—usually much less than the expected life of your house.

These components, of course, will need to be replaced by the house owner at the house owner's expense.

Here is an example of how it works. Standard vinyl windows cost about $250 each, including installation, permits, and disposal, and need replacement every thirty years. So if a home has 20 windows, then windows cost $166 per year ($250 x 20 windows ÷ 30 years = $166). That price is for standard vinyl windows. Wood windows that open four ways and have a decent efficiency rating will cost more. Fancy windows shaped like arches or trapezoids, or exceptionally large windows, or windows with colored or patterned or leaded glass, cost even more.

Another example: basic carpet, padding, installation, haul-away and disposal costs about $15 per square yard and, according to the manufacturer, such carpet needs replacement every eight years. So if your home has 100 square yards of carpeting, the carpet costs $187.50 per year. If you have more carpet than that, or better carpet, the cost goes up.

An average asphalt-shingle roof on a 1,500-square-foot house will cost around $10,000, including tear off, installation, and hauling away the tons of debris. That roof needs to be replaced every 25 years. So your average roof will cost $400 per year for 25 years. Unless your house is larger. Or has complicated architectural features like turrets or dormers or multiples levels and wings. Or the roofing material is cedar shake, or tile, or metal. Then the costs go up.

Now multiply these sorts of numbers by all the parts of your house.

Our Replacement Table applies this accounting to most everything substantial that needs to be replaced over time in the aver-

Discount components like this 17.5 year door can throw off your calculations

age house. For the sake of brevity we will ignore smaller items like door knobs and switch & outlet covers.

If you buy a house, however, you won't be able to ignore these myriad smaller items. They will belong to you and you will pay to replace them when they are broken or embarrassingly outdated. You'll pay to replace garden hose water valves, motion sensors, closet door tracks, various and sundry plumbing fittings, bits of trim, soffit and fascia, cabinet knobs and hinges, shrubs and bushes, heater vents, vent covers, shelves, stair tread, broken windows, fireplace grates, solar lights, outdoor turf, tool sheds, paper towel and toilet paper holders, fences and gates, thermostats, door bells, chimney caps, drawer slides, porch lights, paint, caulk and adhesive, *etcetera, ad nauseum*.[25]

Remember: outdated knobs are like a ticking time bomb.

Below the Replacement Table is our Repair and Maintenance Costs Table. This lists house parts that require regular maintenance. A house owner is required to undertake regular maintenance by the mortgage holder, insurance company(ies), and, under threat of voiding warranties, the various installers and manufacturers of all the parts needing service. Local codes and/or the Home Owners Association (HOA) will also have mandates about your house's maintenance and upkeep.

This all means that, in the end, if you don't keep up with your house replacement, repair, and maintenance costs you could face serious consequences.

Consequences like voided warranties, lost property value, administrative or legal action from a nosy HOA or Community Association, tickets or fines from your local municipality, and possible liability under the concept of waste, which means you made your Big Banking Business friends sad by allowing the house they helped you buy to fall apart. Not to mention divorce from a spouse who is tired of wading through pools of fetid water on the way to your broken shower.

This list of items in the Replacement Table is designed to be demonstrative. There might be items on this list that wouldn't be applicable to you. Maybe you don't need air conditioning or a sump pump. On the other hand, maybe you need a swamp cooler, or a big doggy fence, or a pole barn or solarium. Overall, this is a pretty good representation of the kinds of expenses you'll be staring down if you own a house.

---

[25] With these two Latin terms we have fulfilled our requirements under the "Educational Book Minimum Latin Requirement Act."

Replacement Table

Component	Approximate Life	Cost to Replace	Figure Used	Annual Cost
Air conditioner(s)	10	$600 - $5,000	$2,500	$250
Bath & shower valves	20	$100 - $300	($200 x 3)	$20
Cabinets, bath	30	$1,500 - $3,000	($2,000 x 2 sets)	$133
Cabinets, kitchen	30	$5,000 - $12,000	$7,500	$250
Carpet	8	$1,500 - $3,500	$2,000	$250
Compactor	6	$250 - $500	$350	$58
Counter tops	15	$1,500 - $4,500	$2,000	$133
Deck	20	$1,500 - $10,000	$3,500	$175
Dehumidifier	8	$,200 - $500	$300	$37
Dishwasher	8	$500 - $1,200	$700	$87
Doors (interior)	30+	$159 - $300	($200 x 10)	$66
Doors (slider)	20	$600 - $2,500	$1,200	$50
Doors (exterior)	30	$500 - $900	$600	$20
Driveway (asphalt)	20	$2,000 - $3,000	$2,000	$100
Dryer	10	$300 - $800	$450	$45
Electrical circuit box	20	$900	$900	$45
Electric wiring	30	$3,000 - $5,000	$4,000	$133
Electric switches & plugs	20	$2,000	$2,000	$100
Fans (bath)	15	$100 - $200	$100 x 2	$13
Fans (ceiling)	15	$250 - $400	$250 x 2	$33
Faucets	15	$60 - $300	$150 x 3	$30
Flooring (non carpet)	20	$1,000 - $2,500	$2,000	$100
Freezer	11	$350 - $1,000	$500	$45
Furnace or boiler	20	$3,000 - $8,000	$4,500	$225
Garage door & opener	15	$1,000 - $2,000	$1,500	$100
Garbage disposal	8	$100 - $300	$200	$25
Gutters	20	$1,200 - $2,500	$1,800	$90
Humidifier	15	$200 - $700	$250	$16
Light fixtures (indoor)	15	$50 -$150	$75 x 10	$50
Light fixtures (outdoor)	10	$100 - $150	$100 x 3	$30
Microwave	8	$250 - $600	$350	$43
Mailbox	15	$60 - $200	$125	$8
Paint (interior)	12	$1,200 - $2,000	$1,500	$125
Paint (exterior)	8	$1,000 - $2,500	$2,000	$250

Component	Approximate Life	Cost to Replace	Figure Used	Annual Cost
Humidifier	15	$200 - $700	$250	$16
Light fixtures (indoor)	15	$50 -$150	$75 x 10	$50
Light fixtures (outdoor)	10	$100 - $150	$100 x 3	$30
Microwave	8	$250 - $600	$350	$43
Mailbox	15	$60 - $200	$125	$8
Paint (interior)	12	$1,200 - $2,000	$1,500	$125
Paint (exterior)	8	$1,000 - $2,500	$2,000	$250
Plumbing	30	$2,000 - $5,000	$3,500	$116
Range (gas or electric)	15	$450 - $1,100	$650	$43
Refrigerator	10	$600 - $2,500	$1,500	$150
Roof	20	$6,000 - $10,000`	$7,000	$350
Security system	8	$1,200 - $3,000	$1,200	$15
Shower enclosure	25	$1,200 - $3,500	$1,500 x 2	$120
Sinks	20	$300 - $600	$400 x 3	$60
Smoke alarms	6	$40 - $60	$50 x 5	$41
Sump pump	10	$200 - $350	$250 x 2	$50
Washer	10	$400 - $900	$650	$65
Water heater	10	$400 - $900	$550	$55
Water softener	10	$450 - $1,500	$1,200	$120
Well pump	15	$1,000 - $2,200	$1,5000	$150
Well	20	$2,500 - $5,000	$3,500	$175
Windows	25	$250 - $400	$300 x 15	$180
TOTAL ANNUAL COST				$4575

Replacement Table Notes

This isn't an exhaustive list. (You're paying for information and bad humor, not walls of text.) No one wants to read the entire assembly kit for a house. We're just trying to make a point. Note that for each item like a "furnace" there are other affiliated items like ductwork, air quality controls, thermostats, floor registers, venting, etc., that will eventually need replacement. A house is just a big pile of mismatched bits each always striving to disintegrate.

Manufacturers give life expectancy based on "first owner use." That's a nice way of saying that if you pay for a $6,000 boiler you'll treat it better than the people you sell the house to. That also means components already installed when you bought your house might not last as long as this list predicts. On the other hand,

Replacement Table Notes

maybe you're comfortable keeping the 40-year-old shag carpeting in the rumpus room for another ten years. Again, consider this list a general guide.

We assume 30 year house ownership—the life of your mortgage—just like the house pushers recommend. If you buy a 20-plus year old house and keep it for 30 years, you may confront the aging-out of some longer life components. What components can wear out after 30 years? Wood. Engineered wood structures. Baseboard systems. Slate roofing. Stucco. Even those fancy copper gutters and hardwood windows might fail. After 50 years, you can even start expecting poured concrete and cast iron and cement blocks to fail in some conditions. *Everything* that makes up a house has a shelf life.

> *Remember that study by online house finders, Zillow? The previously quoted $9,500 in "hidden costs" was an average price. That implies that half of the house owners out there might have higher costs. Our $200,000 example is higher than the average cost for an existing home. The study also cites annual costs over $12,000 in Chicago, and over $13,000 in San Fransisco and Boston.*

To be fair, we used costs for mid-priced items that would be typical for a $200,000 house. No $12,000 Sub-Zero™ refrigerators or $8,000 Jenn-Air™ ranges. Also, no $199 Discount Al's™ dishwashers or second-hand toilets. You won't get two-story-high, triple pane, argon-filled, mahogany Pella™ windows for the $300 per unit that we quote. We aren't figuring on you building your own cheapo windows from Plexiglas and duct tape, either.

If you feel you need titanium and gold toilet fixtures or mahogany cabinet doors, don't expect the lifespan of the item to go up significantly—just assume that your costs will. If you decide to replace your appliances with used stuff from your cousin, well, good luck with that and remember: when you sell the house the mismatched avocado-and-brown kitchen will hurt your resale value.

House builders and suppliers like to pretend everyone uses super premium materials--cultured marble or natural stone counter tops, copper gutters, imported rain forest hardwoods, etc.— and so it was difficult to get accurate answers about the real-life materials most of us have in our houses. Yet we managed. In your research if you see life expectancies higher than the ones in these tables double check to see that they're not based upon titanium and mahogany. Paying three times as much for material to get, maybe, a 50% increase in life span doesn't gain you anything. Worse, many "premium" materials have a shorter life expectancy and are more expensive to maintain.

Our costs assume you'll hire someone to install most of these items. If you choose to assume you'll do the replacement yourself, then remember to consider the cost of a huge list of expensive house repair tools and equipment, material, disposal, permits, delivery, cleanup, etc. Plus, account for 10% to 30% extra for all your material waste and mistakes. Everyone makes mistakes. But you'll pay full price for them.

Also remember that many HOAs and municipalities prohibit house owners from doing much of this work, or possibly any of this work. If a service or repair is dangerous and/or involves hazardous materials; a special license and training is required. If you get caught releasing oil or asbestos or contaminants or refrigerant into the wild you'll be facing bigger problems than hiring a service person.

Don't try running natural gas lines if you're clueless. Do you know where you will put three tons of shingles or a few hundred pounds of wet drywall? What will you do with the old refrigerator or air conditioning unit and their heavily regulated coolants? How do you handle 240/120v of service power? Do you know the safety protocols for handling these items? Do you really want to learn about them through trial and error? We didn't think so. Don't plan your finances around the deadly and impossible.

If you find the cost estimates in this table shocking and unbelievable, we don't blame you. Whoa! Scary stuff. So you'll be glad to know that we have yet another source for cost estimates. The newest house parasite industry: House Warranty Plans. *"For only dollars a day you can protect your house! And all of its fragile, overpriced parts!"*

If you think our numbers are scary, go take a look at what these ~~shysters~~ entrepreneurs claim repair and replacements will cost you. Their cost estimates are as much as *30% to 50% higher* than the ones we use. That makes their cost estimates as much as ten times as expensive as the numbers the house pushers use when they try to convince you house buying is *tré* cool. How can that be?

Is it because the house warranty people are incompetent and clueless regarding costs of their own business? That doesn't seem to make sense. Is it because they're only interested in taking your money? We don't know that and can't say.[26] It could certainly be that they are profit seeking and not focused on saving you money. But they still need information to run their business, don't they?

On the other hand, maybe it's the house warranty folks who are grounded and in touch and—again—it is the house-pushers who are ignoring the truth. One thing for sure: it can't both be true that a house will only cost 1% of the value per year to repair, and at the same time you risk losing "tens of thousands" each year.

---

26 These are metaphysical questions we are not qualified to answer.

We can't mention one of the best examples of these house warranty ~~schemes~~ plans because these folks base their very high, very precise (down to the penny) cost estimates on a fancy survey that they won't share, and forbid us from even mentioning. So we won't mention it. We won't. Except to note that if we could mention this super-secret survey we'd likely opine that it's probably made-up from whole cloth and tilted like a palm tree in a hurricane toward scaring people into buying ~~overpriced~~ house warranty plans. But since we can't mention it, there's no way to know for sure what we might have to say.

The cost estimates we use are much lower than the shrill scare tactics of the house warranty people and even more reasonable than the numbers from the Zillow® study we mentioned while still accounting for a realistic assessment of costs as presented by the parts and service people who set the prices and consumer and insurance experts.

In other words, our numbers are fair.

Repairs and Maintenance

Almost everything that moves or operates or functions or even exists in a house requires at least some routine work. Pretty much everything outside a house does as well.

Mechanical devices need regular checkups, adjustments, or infusions of replaceable parts. Your HVAC needs TLC for igniters, burners, pumps, fans, fittings, valves, gages, compressors, etc. Did you know you need to lubricate garage door tracks? Is your oven level? Where is your water supply main valve and have you checked it twice this year in case of emergency? The refrigerator door water dispenser filter needs regular replacement too. Have you checked the date on your fire extinguishers... you do have fire extinguishers, don't you?

Non-mechanical but working systems need care as well. Gutters must be kept clean or they will fill with debris, water will overflow, and the roof will rot away. Fireplaces must be regularly cleaned and the brick lining repaired. Lack of regular care and/or planting the wrong sorts of landscaping nearby will stop up your sewer drain, necessitating repairs that can cost as much as a good used car.

Even more mundane components of a house need care or they will shuffle off this mortal coil even more quickly than they're designed to do (and in a more expensive and dangerous fashion). A house requires someone to wash the mold and debris off the shingles, clean the range hood filter, lubricate door locks and hinges, clean out the ductwork, test and replace circuit breakers, cover and uncover air conditioners and vent fans according to the season (and make sure wasps or spiders or chipmunks haven't built homes in these places), watch expensive trees and shrubs for signs of disease and damage, listen for problems with bath fans and garbage disposals and other moving parts.

In fact, most everything needs generalized hands-on maintenance: Tightening loose stuff. Loosening tight stuff. Snooping around and looking for trouble. Opening the stopped-up. Stopping-up unwanted openings. Painting. Caulking. Scooping out. Pulling apart. Picking up what fell off.

Houses also require that someone devote a ridiculous and frustrating amount of time to running back and forth to the lumber company, landscape supply house, hardware store, specialty outlets, tool rental company, and landfill or transfer station.

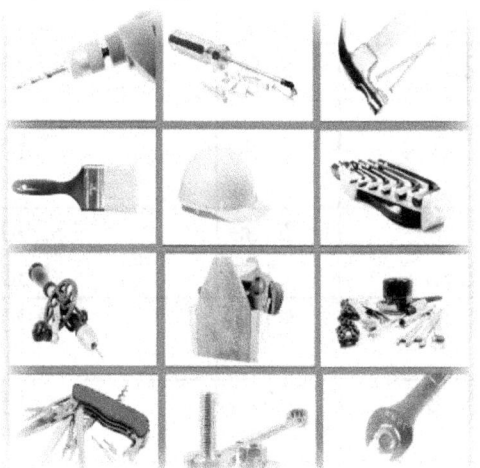

All of this work requires a house owner to either call for expensive service or try to DIY. DIY isn't free. DIY still means the purchase of (expensive) specialized tools, lubricants, seals, measuring devices, and, most importantly, parts. Lots of parts. Plus the expense to dispose of broken stuff.

A DIY house owner needs to account not only for the money but for all the time spent on such projects. These aren't "chores" like taking out the trash or washing dishes that can be justified as part of everyday life. These are extra work, and lots of it, and let's not fool ourselves about the end result: keeping a house from falling apart is not creating income.

Much repair and maintenance has a learning curve, so time must be spent figuring out how to preform each task. Each task takes longer to perform until it's perfected. Since many tasks are not performed often enough to allow a house owner to reach any level of competence, each one becomes a slow series of bumbling, half-remembered steps: *"Which ladder do I need for cleaning out the gutters? Where is it? Who planted all these flowering shrubs right where I have to put the ladder to reach the tallest part of the house? Where is that little gutter-cleaning gadget? Why isn't this garden hose working?"*

Or: *"Hey! Where is that tool for removing the furnace filter? Who moved it!? Why are there three different filter sizes written on the outside of the cover?? Which circuit breaker do I shut off to kill the power…dammit! There goes the router and alarm again!"*

Repair and Maintenance Table

Component	Interval	Cost to service	Figure used	Cost per	Annual cost
Air conditioner(s)	Yearly	$100 - $200	$120	$120	$120
Carpet	Semi-annual	$100 - $300	$100	$400	$200
Deck(s)	Bi-annual	$150 - $300	$200	$100	$200
Dehumidifier	Annual	$45 - $70	$50	$50	$50
Driveway (asphalt)	Annual	$45 - $500	$200	$200	$200
Driveway {concrete)	Bi-annual	$200 - $400	$300	$150	$150
Dryer	Annual	$25 - 150	$75	$75	$75
Faucet(s)	One per year	$25 - $100	$50	$50	$50
Filters (assorted)	Annual or more often	$25 - $150	$ 25 x 4	$100	$100
Fire extinguishers	Annual	$10 - $50	$20 x 4	$100	$80
Fireplace	Annual	$199 - $299	$199	$199	$250
Freezer	Annual	$45 - $100	$50	$50	$50
Furnace or Boiler	Annual	$79 - $200	$100	$100	$100
Garage door & Opener	Annual	$25 - $100	$25	$25	$25
Garbage Disposal	Semi-Annual	$15	$15	$15	$30
Gutters	Annual	$50 - $100	$75	$75	$75
Humidifier	Semi-annual	$20	$20	$40	$40
Lawn & trim	Weekly in season	$25 - $50	$30 x 35 weeks	$1050	$1050
Lawn treat & fertilize	As needed	$250	$250	$250	$250
Leaves (remove)	As needed	$75 - $150	$75 x 2	$150	$150
Paint (interior)	Yearly	$30 - $100	$50	$50	$50
Paint (exterior)	Yearly	$20 - $100	$50	$50	$50
Refrigerator	Annual	$20 - $100	$30	$30	$30
Roof	Annual	$25 - $200	$100	$100	$100

Repair and Maintenance Table

Component	Interval	Cost to service	Figure used	Annual cost
Smoke alarms	Annual	$20 - $50	$25	$25
Snow Removal	Annual contract	$250 - $500	$250	$250
Sump Pump	Annual	$50 - $100	$75	$75
Trees & Shrubs	Annual	$100 - $300	$150	$150
Washer	Bi-Annual	$50 - $100	$100	$50
Water Softener	Quarterly	$25	$25	$100
Well & Pump	Annual	$100 - $200	$100	$100
Misc Caulk & Gaskets & Seals & Trim	Constant	$10 - $50 [x many]	$100	$100
TOTAL				$4185

Fun Facts!

Burst washing machine hoses are among the top insurance claims, averaging between $4,000 and $6,000 in damages. A burst hose can pump up to 650 gallons of water per hour into your house

House-related accidents cause 21 million injuries and over 20,000 deaths each year in the US.

Clogged dryer vents cause over 9,000 house
fires every year.

Modern washing machines are efficient and safe for clothes, but very complex. Replacing the tub can cost more than a new washer

Maintenance Table Notes

Just as with the Replacement Table, there are likely some expenses on this Maintenance Table that won't apply to you and others you will encounter that have been left off. We've tried to be fair and skew to the low end of potential expenses and their frequency. Lawn care can easily hit four figures if you have a big exurban lot or fruit trees and a garden or a demanding HOA. Wells can be nightmares. Older furnaces can be very expensive. Water leaks or electric and plumbing repairs can require a loan. Even caulk and paint and tools start becoming a separate budget item in your household expenses.

> **My favorite neighbor.** *"My favorite neighbor is actually a lesbian couple and their grown hellspawn college aged kids. The women were recently arrested for defrauding an 80 year old man out of his life savings, nearly $100k, by befriending him and posing as his "caretakers." One is currently in prison, and the other violated probation and is a fugitive. The rest of the family (their deadbeat kids and I guess their friends?) still live there, and apparently have been selling weed and/or meth to make the mortgage payments. There are constantly strange cars parked illegally in our cul de sac, and it's a nice, expensive neighborhood with the exception of them. So it f*cking sucks that I have to be paranoid about my property when my house was far from cheap. No one wants to complain to the cops out of fear they'd retaliate by trying to kill pets or something."*

As previously noted, and repeated, we've listed the cost to have a professional do the work. If you plan to do all this work yourself then you're delusional. ~~Few people~~ No one can safely service an air conditioner, properly prune a fruit tree, remove snow before work each morning, clean their own gutters, power wash and re-stain their own deck, service a gas-fired boiler or furnace, replace broken glass, hard wire the new smoke alarms, etc., and still hold a job to pay for all of it.

But if you stubbornly decide to try to go that route remember you'll still pay a significant part of the cost, plus you'll need a large collection of specialized tools (a/c leak detectors and recharge equipment, a collection of ladders for indoor and outdoor use, power equipment like mowers and blowers, a set of mechanics' tools, another set of carpenter's tools, etc.) Don't dismiss this list of costs until and unless you've replaced our numbers with thousands of dollars in tools and equipment and estimates of time and disposal costs.

Also, don't forget to budget for all the hours it will take you to learn to do all these things on a regular basis, and as needed. Cancel your vacation(s).

> Replacement: $4,575 per year
> Maintenance: $4,185 per year
> TOTAL $8,760 per year

You may have noticed that some costs appear on the Replacement Table and also on the Maintenance Table. Yes they do. One of the sad truths about complex systems like houses and cars is that we tend to throw money at them right up to the point when we give up. So it is common to pay for one or two or even three service calls on that old refrigerator or washer just before giving up and then spending even more money to replace it.[27] Such is life.

Notice that $8,760 *is bigger than* $2,000 ($2,000 is the "one percent of the price of the house" estimate the house pushers use).

By now maybe you've gone through these lists with a red pencil scratching off items: *"Let's see," I don't have a sump pump or a security system. I'm going to steal a lawn mower from the neighbors who are out of town. I'll take out the smoke detectors and the ceiling fans too. I'll board up that extra bathroom. And the damned caulk can take care of itself! So I'd be looking at lower costs, right?"*

Oh yeah. I've cut my costs in half.

Yes, most likely you would. Kinda of. For a while. We'll leave you ponder, though, how those modifications might influence your resale value, your warranty standing, your mortgage and insurance obligations not to mention or your ability to live safely in a house over the long term. Plus, hey, if you are going to live like a Dickens character, why buy house?

No matter how much we quibble with any particular expense, after looking at these long lists of upkeep costs it's clear there's no way the grand total can add up only to the "one percent of value" house pushers assume.

The real take away here is the sheer number of house components to replace, repair, or maintain, and their predictable and inevitable costs. All the parts of a house need upkeep, all have a shelf life. All their associated costs are the responsibility of a house owner. They are manifold and expensive.

While a house owner is unlikely to spend $8,000 every year on house upkeep, it could happen this year. Every house owner has had a few of those seasons. All is going well then: bang! A sewer line blockage, or roof leak, or the garage door falls on the car. Suddenly the vacation fund is gone, the credit card is maxed out, and selling pets to pay repair bills becomes a viable option.

Many house owners can tell you grave and disturbing stories of even worse years. Uninsured basement

---

27 As this was being written a friend told a story about paying for a $1,600 emergency repair for an old furnace in the dead of winter, just a few months before having the furnace replaced/upgraded for another $5,200.

floods. Pest infestations. The need to replace an entire house full of electrical or plumbing systems. Insurance doesn't cover many expenses, even the sorts of accidents and disasters we don't list in the tables, and even covered expenses have deductibles and "out of pocket costs" that you'll be raiding the piggy bank to cover. *Plus* maintenance and replacing parts and systems.

If you, the reader, want to base your financial future on the assumption that your $200,000 house will only cost $2,000 in replacement, maintenance, and repairs each year (less than one quarter of our conservative prediction) you're free to do that. It would be pretty irresponsible to do that, but you can if you chose. You'd be contradicting the estimates used by appliance and systems manufacturers, retailers, repair services and the insurance data, not to mention the house warranty folks. In other words, you'd be choosing to use the estimates created solely for the purpose of selling you a house as opposed to the estimates based on facts. But go right ahead. We're just giving you information.

Meanwhile, back in the real world, the rest of us need to move forward with the discussion and the book.

For the purpose of our ongoing cost accumulation, we'll assume a very reasonable 2% ($5,000) spent per year in potential replacement, maintenance and repairs. ($5,000 x 30 years = $150,000.)

Mortgage:	$342,456
PMI:	$ 14,100
Taxes	$ 75,000
Insurance	$ 45,000
Repair & Replace	$150,000
Cost of $200,000 house:	$626,565

If you'll glance out of the port-side windows you'll see that we're now well past the half-million dollar mark. Let's circle the metaphorical plane and finish this up.

Luxury Costs

Our Luxury Costs Table reflects additional costs for components that houses don't need, but which make life within them worth living. Add-ons like pools, spas, gardens, patios, and man (or woman) caves. Huge secret underground lairs. Stuff like that.

Some may call them extravagances, but to a sophisticated person such as the average American house buyer they feel more like well-deserved rewards for hard work and smart decision making. Who doesn't dream of a personal cider press? Who would purposefully want to crush that dream?

A house owner's ability to buy and install and use these things is a key talking point of the house pushers. Enjoying wi-fi equipped fenced dog runs and tiki bars with built in BBQ smokers and two-story tree houses with wall to wall carpet is supposed to be one of the major motivations for wanting to buy a house, remember?

And really, why the hell not? If house owners are going to be shackled for 30 years to $626,565 (so far)[28] in house costs, they might as well drop a bit more money to enjoy the ride. Right? Get some throw pillows for the cell? A few tunes for the highway to hell?

If you are like most people thinking of buying a house you've envisioned a few of these things gracing your life.

Most house owners are willing to pay for at least some of these extravagances. And pay, pay, pay they do!

> My favorite neighbor: *"Blower Dude" as the whole family refers to him. When we moved in he told us none of the neighbors got along with him (gee, wonder why?) and then said since there were no deciduous trees on his property he would be blowing any leaves that fell into his yard over our fence. Okay. This guy used his leaf blower 4-5 times a day. He would spend hours carefully blowing the snow off his chain link fence while it was still snowing. Wanna sleep in? You'll have to make it through his two backyard passes before 10am, so good luck. It should be better in summer right? Nope, this guy actually mowed his lawn every single day, sometimes multiple times a day. Wish I were kidding. He got too sick to mow the summer before he died and would sit on his back porch watching his poor 30-year-younger wife doing it and yelling about how wrong she did it till he finally dropped dead."*

---

28 So far. We aren't finished yet.

Luxury Cost Table

Potential luxury	Buy/Install	Figure used	Maintenance per year	Power cost per year	Lifespan	Cost per year
Basketball court	$4,000 - $15,000	$5,000	$50	$50	-	$667
Built-in grill/ BBQ	$5,000 - $15,000	$7.500	$75	$10	40	$370
Garden (large)	$500 - $2,500	$600	$200	$50	-	$520
Garden (small)	$100 - $500	$200	$100	$20	-	$126
Gazebo	$2,500 - $4,600	$3,000	$40	-	-	$140
Greenhouse	$500 - $5,000	$1,500	$100	$0 - $500	-	$116
Home workshop	$1,000 - $5,000	$1,500	$50	$25	-	$160
Kennel	$$1,500 - $3,000	$1,800	50	$0 - $100	-	$90
Media Room	$2,500 - $8,000	$4,000	$100	$60	5 - 8	$660
Outbuilding (large)	$5,000 - $20,000	$8,000	$200	$300	-	$766
Outbuilding (small)	$1,500 - $8,000	$4,000	$100	-	-	$233
Playplace	$1,000 - $10,000	$2,000	$50	-	20	$150
Pool (in ground)	$14,000 - $21,000	$18,000	$499	$50 - $200	-	$2,000
Pool (above ground)	$3,500 - $5,000	$4,000	$350	$75 - $150	15 - 20	$1,816
Pond	$500 - $5,000	$41,500	$150	$0 - $120	-	$50
Spa/Hot tub	$3,500 = $10,000	$4,500	$300	$40 - $100	15	$650
Tennis Court	$50,000 - $80,000	$65,000	$1,500	$0 - $120	-	$2,216
Waterfall	$500 - $5,000	$1,500	$300	$25 - $100	-	$330
TOTAL						$11,060

Luxury Cost Table Notes

Before you pull out your red pen to start critiquing our estimates, note that this table just touches on the potential costs of some of these fun and tasty items. Almost every one of these luxuries can cost up to ten times this much depending upon where you live and just how much fun you want to have.

Northern Minnesota folks who insist on a heated outdoor spa? Prepare for higher bills. Live near Tempe but absolutely have to have a 20,000 gallon pool or huge, water-sucking garden? If so, then expect your costs to shame those in this modest little chart and make it blush.

Each of these projects can require permits, raise your taxes, raise your insurance costs, and involve tear-down, disposal and delivery fees.

Also note that each and every one of these items can also have an ongoing energy cost if they involve lighting, heat, cooling, power or music, though we give many of them a $0 cost. Again, we have made a conscious decision to use reasonable estimates.

Note especially that _we're not even including_ anything _from this category_ in our ongoing accounting of costs. Not one dime for pools or hot tubs or helipads.

If you consider throwing caution to the wind and start down the self-destructive path of house financing, you may want to handle this differently than we have. You may want to budget for a media room or heated workshop or whatever extra you feel you need. After all, you are promising yourself to stick by your pile of SPF and OSB for 30 years. Do you plan to forgo such luxuries for the rest of your life?

But we are trying to cut the house pushers as much slack so we won't count _any_ of these predictable costs. We're just going to leave this category here for you to ponder.

Mortgage:	$342,456
PMI:	$ 14,100
Taxes	$ 75,000
Insurance	$ 45,000
Repair & Replace	$150,000
~~Potential Luxuries~~	~~$331,800~~ $0 (Not counted)
~~Cost of $200,000 house:~~	~~$928,365~~
Cost of $200,000 house:	$626,565

Upgrades: "Spruce Up Your House for Summer!"[29]

The more time we spend pulling apart the pro-house talking points, the more we find the math is making little sense even by their rules.

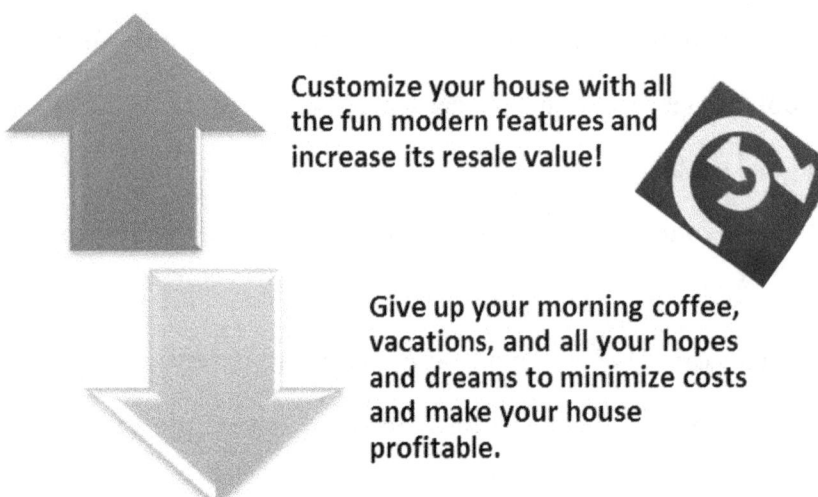

One of the most common reasons given for owning a house is so that buyers can "make it their own." Paint! Landscape! Install granite counter tops! Add a central vacuum! A Jacuzzi! A sauna! Install a 1000-square-foot media/game room with smell-o-vision! Equip a custom kitchen with designer appliances connected to the Internet and an alarm system that can launch the entire house into orbit if Yellowstone finally blows! Don't forget the martial arts workout room, a custom designed office for a work-at-home professional, two indoor pools and a Bat Cave!

Oddly, another of the other most common reasons given for owning a home is how much money you might save/make just by paying your mortgage payments. "Why throw your money away on rent?" "Put your money to work for you!" The house pushers have even taken to suggesting you "skip your morning latte" and put the money toward owning a house. The implication: you're only a couple of double-tall-soys away from financial freedom. [Damn you caffeine!]

While both of these reasons (freedom to customize and the desire to be frugal) are important to justify the purchase of a house, they're mutually exclusive—even at odds. "Spend money on gold-plated ceiling fans" versus "give up coffee to save, save, save!"

Given the ridiculously small margins that the house pushers use to support buying, you can't "make money" on a house if you're constantly spending your tax returns and birthday money on heated garage floors and lighted roof-top gazebos.

---

29 The first house improvement ad we found at random

On the other hand, one of the most critical aspects of "making money" with a house is the necessity that the house be worth a lot more 30 years hence than you paid for it now. If you buy a $200,000 house and it's only worth $200,000 at the end of 30 years then you, my friend, have made a serious mistake by anyone's accounting.

So the house-pushing examples always predict some amazing rate of value increase over time. "At the end of 30 years your $200,000 house will be worth $810,000!" They need this impressive and completely ridiculous value increase for their math to work.[30]

Implied in this value increase is a modern, up-to-date, desirable house. No one is going to pay top-dollar for a house with a coal stove and built-in 8 track player. Have you made any offers on houses with ice boxes instead of refrigerators? Would you look at anything with a "cute and quaint" outhouse rather than 2.5 baths?

If we can only budget 1% of the house's value per year for upgrades, how are we going to afford to pull down the stables and build a heliport for our new flying car? In the real world, the flying car wins. People who are still using their 40-year-old appliances 40 years later are so rare they merit media comment and YouTube videos. As fun as it is to marvel at pink, steam-powered refrigerators and vintage paneling, we all know that these folks are screwed when it comes to resale value. Most of us spend a whole lot of money on updates and upgrades.[31]

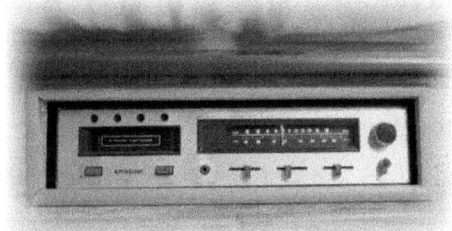

The previous owners upgraded from their Victrola to this 8-track player. It even comes with some T-Rex and MC5 tapes!

In fact, the home improvement industry estimates that house owners spend at least six times as much on "upgrades" as renters. Not surprising. Most renters aren't interested in installing heated indoor pools or home elevators: they (like landlords) tend to make common sense upgrades like paint and new carpet. Even if renters were interested, many renters aren't allowed to make expensive changes (though we can imagine

---

30 Yale economist and America's "foremost expert on house values," Robert Shiller, estimates that house values have gone up only an average of 0.2% a year over the past 100 years. Not the ridiculous 4% to 6% house pushers claim.

31 Laugh if you want. In 30 years your edgy granite counters and stainless steel appliances will prompt rude laughter and pointing from your grandkids. Wait and see

that few landlords would protest if their tenant wanted to spring for a marble floors.) But house owners can and do upgrade. If they want their house to hold its value—much less increase—they have no choice. This is such a predictable and lucrative market that entire national chains of stores and service franchises exist, and profit, solely from house owners' desire to dump money into fancy new stuff.

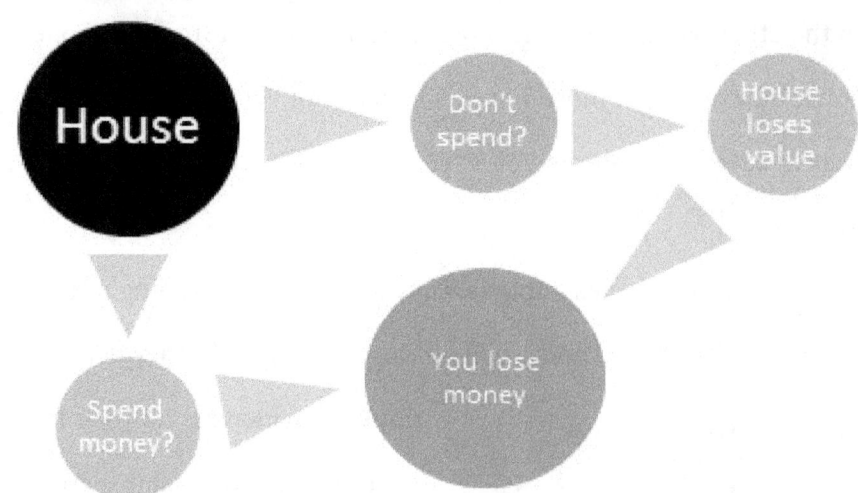

The Magic Cycle of house upkeep and upgrade.

What's your house-desire? How are the people on the TV shows pimping their cribs?

A fire pit in your pool? A door that turns into a ping pong table? A trap door wine cellar in your kitchen? A built in TV for the bathtub? A bone shaped basin for your dog? Extend-able balcony? Two-story walk-in closet? Creek running under your hallway? Secret rooms? Do the neighbors have one? Eeek!! Are they putting such things in new builds? Will my house seem hopelessly outdated without a WiFi equipped robotic toilet paper dispenser? (Of course it will!)

All this and more is available. For a price.

According to that monitor of all things expensive—American Express—*house owners will spend an average of $4000 a year on upgrades.*[32] Not repair. Not maintenance. Just on upgrades.

Well, of course we will! We're "consumers," after all.

"*Consumers are investing in their homes this year across nearly every category from DIY to new home furnishings,*" said a senior vice president of American Express. "*Whether they're redoing one room or the whole house, there is a significant bump in spending that should bode well for many merchants.*[33]"

Well, of course it will. Lucky merchants. And don'cha love the use of the word "investing?" Because every electric tie rack and motion activated faucet has an 8% ROI.

---

[32] That cost alone is twice the house-pushers estimate, as well as being as large as our entire budget for upkeep and maintenance.

[33] Interview with "houselogic.com"

Realize, too, that if the average house owner is spending $4,000 on house upgrades this year, that means half are spending even more!

American Express isn't alone in keeping a sharp eye on our money pits. According to the money meisters at <u>Forbes</u>, the folks over at Houzz.com[34] have completed "the largest survey of renovation and decorating activity ever conducted." Whoa. That's historic!

Turns out, the self-selected folks who take surveys at Houzz will spend an average of $28,030 on kitchen remodels and $10,422 on bathroom renovations this year. Holy cow! That seems like a bit more than $2,000 doesn't it?

Just so we don't miss an additional point, a representative from Houzz breaks it down for us. "A majority of homeowners planning major home renovation or decoration projects in the next two years are also planning to hire professional help."

He said that for the benefit of all you folks who picture yourself in Bob Vila plaid with a miter saw crafting a wine cellar in your spare time.

Another bit of shocking news from <u>Forbes</u>/Houzz: "The majority of renovation projects exceed initial budgets." Well, who could have predicted that?

Even more encouraging news for those who profit from (other people's) house owning: House owners are "more likely to cut back in other areas, such as vacations and other big-ticket purchases, than delay or decrease their budget for home plans." Because who needs life-changing travel, priceless family memories or a working kidney when it's possible to upgrade your vanity with concrete?

If we take these professional money trackers at their word, $4,000 per year over 30 years means the average house owner will spend $120,000 on built-in wine coolers, geo-thermal hydraulic doggy doors and other upgrades to current systems and house components. There goes more potential house "profit."

Honey, do you realize we could have upgraded all of our vanities to concrete for what this trip cost?

---

34 Houzz: "We're a platform for home remodeling and design, bringing homeowners and home professionals together in a uniquely visual community."

To skew things even more in the house-pushers favor, we'll only use half of the expert estimate of upgrades in our budget. That seems pretty conservative. $2,000 per year. $2,000 x 30 years = $60,000.

Mortgage:	$342,456
PMI:	$ 14,100
Taxes	$ 75,000
Insurance	$ 45,000
Repair & Replace	$150,000
~~Luxury extras~~	~~$ 60,000~~ $0 (Not counted)
Upgrades	$ 60,000
Cost of $200,000 house:	$671,565

Just remember, dear readers: if you don't budget enough for home upgrades you'll likely never be able to sell your aging pile of antiques for anywhere near its potential value (which isn't all that much to begin with).

Lord of the Land

Land means many things. Land is dirt. That means filth, dust, mud, weeds, lawn care, rodents, insects, sidewalks, driveways, curbs, trees, fences, encroaching animals, landscaping, and a myriad of other problems too overwhelming to list in one sentence. Your little piece of the pie.

Land is also a bunch of abstract responsibilities. That means trespassers, zoning issues, taxes, easements, code enforcement, millages, liability, utilities, riparian rights, rights of way, mandatory upkeep, and possibly a rabid and power-hungry Homeowners Association.[35]

Land is another realm of Darwinian competition. Land drafts you into the unenviable game of competing with your miserable peers to see whose mulch is fresher, grass is greener, and driveway edging is straighter.

You'll also be shocked to learn that your small patch of weeds and gravel requires you to purchase enough tools and equipment to run a commercial ranch. Have a large lot or acreage? Your new landscaping and lawn care duties mean that you face much of the labor of owning a farm, with none of the profit potential.

In America every house owner needs his or her own lawn mower, leaf blower, sprinkler system, garden hoses, ladders, cutters, choppers, trimmers, broadcast spreaders, a bewildering array of specialized rakes and shovels, an entire aisle at Home Depot's worth of watering gadgets, and a small piece of tracked diesel powered earthmoving equipment. Ok, maybe not the earthmover. But you're likely to need the rest. And you may need the earthmover.

---

35 We'll be discussing HOAs in more detail later.

Lord of the Land

Is that you, Fido?

If you're unlucky enough to live in the so-called "snow belt" you'll also need snow shovels, a snow blower, ice melt, ice scrapers, a snow plow, equipment for winterizing, installation of eaves trough heat tape, covers for outdoor spigots and irritating little flags on flexible little poles that you'll use to mark your driveway, sidewalks, mailbox, grill, and less-favored pets to help you locate them after they're buried under snow.

Have fruits trees? You need sprayers and pruning equipment, maybe another type of ladder. Pool or spa? You'll need enough equipment for a "volunteer" Russian ~~invasion~~ liberation of a former-Soviet country. Deck? Porch? Gazebo? Carport? Patio? Mulch or compost pile? Fence? Garage? Each can require an expensive specialized set of tools and supplies.

Did you know that the lines that are painted on both tennis and basketball courts require a special type of paint and a special line-painting tool? Of course they do.

If you plant a flower or vegetable garden, consider a second mortgage. Entire retail chains exist to cater exclusively to home gardeners.

You'll want to consider buying a storage shed, too, or your growing pile of tools and equipment will take over your garage and force you to park on the street for the rest of your life. Did you ever wonder why people who own garages park outside?

If you think you'll avoid this expensive fate by forgoing all outdoor endeavors and hiring someone to do your landscaping...don't fool yourself. While you can hire out your yard work, it won't be cheap. Even simple mowing and upkeep contracts can cost as much as tuition to the local community college.

A 2015 article on consumer advocate website Angie's List quoted two lawn services, one estimating a cost of $200 per month, the other $150 per month for simple mowing and edging services in the Midwest.

Real landscaping, on the other hand, is breathtakingly expensive. Stones and turf and sprinklers and walls and fountains can cost as much as a kitchen remodel (if you don't already know, revel in your ignorance and don't even ask us what a kitchen remodel can cost).

Even if you hire a basic landscaping service out of desperation, it won't solve all of your problems. You'll

Hey Kid! Can you mow that spot under the pear tree on your next lap?

still end up buying most all the equipment anyway. For one thing, you'll need it to repair the impressive damage inflicted by speeding teenagers on commercial mowers who actually perform the yard work you contracted from the nice old guy in a John Deere hat.

Plus, someone will have to do (or pay another to do) all the little "extras" that aren't included in the price of your landscaping contract.

"Sure, the cost of cutting the lawn is included. But we had to charge you extra to bring a mower out. You didn't have one. Gas? You don't have gas for the mower? Oooo. Well. Yeah, gonna have to charge you extra for that, too. Sure we said we'd rake your leaves. And we did. Big ol' pile. But we can't haul them away for that price. We piled them up in the driveway. That ok?"

When a storm finally knocks down the big branch over the garage you'll need to find an additional company who specializes in removing big branches from garage roofs. But that service won't pull out the huge, ugly dead shrub that's root bound around your water pipes. Nope. Or fix the fence the neighbors backed into while you were at work, which they've already done three times now, and isn't it just like them to just leave it that way and say nothing?

Nor can you be certain the lawn service will cart away the bushes you trimmed yourself out of desperation because the lawn service never got around to doing it even after the damn things scraped all the paint off your window; scraping and scratching, scratching and scraping, every damned time the wind blows … like fingernails on a chalkboard. Sob!

In fact, the big-branch-over-the-garage service might not even be able or willing to haul away the wood from the big branch they cut. Better verify that before you write them a check...or give them cash because they said they need to get paid in cash. Just like the sump pump guy.

> My favorite neighbor: *"The old lady across the street that's so antisocial that she had her front porch stairs removed. She used to have a bunch of "No trespassing" and "No soliciting" signs posted on her house but then about three years ago she took all of them down and had her concrete stairs removed."*

Second Mortgages

A second mortgage is any loan taken out after the primary mortgage using the house as collateral. These mortgages are also referred to as "home-improvement loans," "junior liens," and "debt-consolidation loans."

Here is the logic. You now need money because you spent all of the money you had previously on interest, taxes, insurance, repairs and the other costs of a house. So you go back and re-borrow money against what little value you've built up in your house by paying off the money you borrowed the first time. More transaction costs follow. More 93% interest payments.

According to Federal Reserve Board data, homeowners took out a total of $2.69 trillion from their houses between 2004 and 2006 (the height of the housing boom).

And according to the Wall Street Journal, of those who took out second mortgages then, 40 percent are now "underwater" on their houses (they owe more than the house is worth). This is more than double the rate of those who didn't take out second mortgages.

Second mortgages might be the most obvious objective evidence available that people who finance houses have masochistic tendencies rather than financial savvy. Hurt me, they're silently begging. Take my money. Take it again.

However, facts are facts. Since most people who finance end up taking out a second mortgage on their houses (62% to 80% of house owners depending upon who you ask) we're going to include a small one in our house buying example.

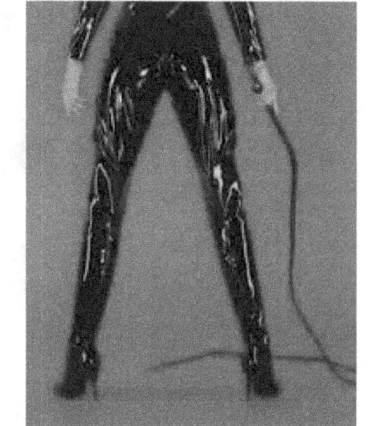

Can you make it an interest only, variable APR, balloon payment loan? Oh Yissss!!

So here are you, our average house buyer, in year 16 of your primary mortgage with all of your cash tied up in property tax payments and lawn treatments. But you need to replace some windows, and really want to add an internet-ready digital fireplace to your kitchen. ~~All the other kids~~…all the other families on the block have one now and you fear your property value will decline if you don't have one, too.

So you scamper over to the bank and borrow $22,000 at 5.5%, canceling out much of the small amount of equity you've built up in your house. This second mortgage will be paid off at closing so it won't run for the full 30 years, but due to the way mortgage loans are structured you'll still owe $21,619.73 even after making $19,840 in payments over 14 years. This means your $22,000 loan carries a total cost of $41,460.

Mortgage:	$342,456
PMI:	$ 14,100
Taxes	$ 75,000
Insurance	$ 45,000
Repair & Replace	$150,000
~~Luxury extras~~	~~$ 60,000~~ $0 (Not counted)
Upgrades	$ 60,000
2nd Mortgage	$ 41,460
Cost of $200,000 house:	$728,024 (so far)

(NOTE: The repair costs paid for by the second mortgage are not being counted in the separate repair cost category but rather are considered as second mortgage costs.)

Closing Costs

Imagine you wander the aisles of your favorite big box store shopping for some gotta-have item. Let's say it's a geo-thermal salad crisper. You compare crispers on the shelf. You pull out your smart phone to search for coupons or discounts and compare online reviews. Search Amazon for a better deal. You decide to curl up and take a quick nap. Finally, you make a decision. You cart your new geo-thermal salad crisper up to the checkout, and the nice young lady with the Celtic face tattoos rings up your purchase, hits you with an upsell for the extended warranty, and finally informs you of "closing costs."

"Closing costs?" you foolishly ask.

"Sure," the checkout woman explains. "You have to pay us for our time and effort. We had to order these salad crispers, have them shipped in, unpack them, and pay someone to ignore you while you took up space in our store comparison shopping. And … um … you took a nap in aisle seven. That was weird, by the way. Plus, I have to stand here and ring up the purchase. I have to make a living too, you know. Face tattoos aren't free."

"But, isn't all that included in the price of the item? Don't you folks mark up the price to pay your overhead?"

The cashier pulls out her nose stud and cleans it on her shirt, "Well, duh," she explains. "We have to make profit. But we also charge you for the costs. Why should *we* pay to ship in this crap you want?"

Most of us would leave the store at this point *sans* gadget. Some of us might even make a caustic remark or two. But for some reason we don't bat an eye when facing the same logic and expenses while buying a house.

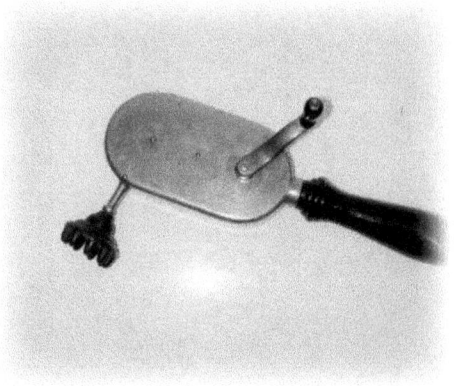

Geo-thermal salad crisper*

After all, so-called closing costs aren't a value-added extra. They also aren't an option. You can't call Gail® at the real estate shop and say tell her you want one medium house, hold the closing costs. These costs are required. But why? Why this substantial expense for house buyers and sellers? Why, in other words, does the mortgage holder make $142,000, Gail® and her ilk make 6% off the top, the repair and supply industry make enough to pay for a nice boat, but you pay all the overhead?

As with everything else house-related, the truth is hidden under layers of BS.

Consumer advocates compare closing costs to the gamesmanship of car dealers. Some dealers will offer you a "guaranteed" trade in for your 1980 Plymouth, but then keep any manufacturer's rebates. Others will give you "cash back" but add a few extra fees and some additional finance charges. At the end of the day they'll all make their money. That's how they can afford those horrible radio commercials featuring stammering family members reading lines like: "I wanna see ya in a Kia!"

But that doesn't really explain why closing costs exist at all. What in the ever-loving hell is a "Document Preparation Fee?" The mortgage company charging $142,000 in interest for a house can't even fill out the necessary paperwork?

"Well, we were caught off guard, Ms. House Buyer, when we heard we'd have to print forms from the hard drive and add your name to them. We've never had such a crazy request before. We managed to make it happen, but we have to charge you."

"Review fees." "Application fees." "Funding fees." "Commitment fees." "Courier fees." "Underwriting fees."

What is all this nonsense? Isn't this sort of thing usually called "running your office?" Will they be passing along the cost of coffee and their electric bill? A "buying-the-receptionist-a-wedding-present fee?"

> * Ok. It really isn't a geo-thermal salad shooter. Its an antique sex toy. This was the only extra image file we had.

Closing Costs

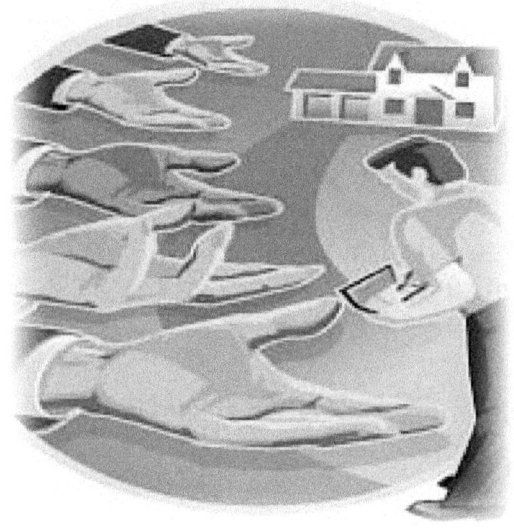

It is tempting to concede somewhat and allow that a few of these fees—an "Appraisal Fee," for instance—might be understandable. Maybe these are outside costs? But then again, wait a minute. Isn't appraisal also a normal, predictable cost of the house-selling business? The finance company wants to know what the house is really worth so they don't mess up and loan $200,000 for a $100,000 house. But isn't that *their* problem and *their* risk? Isn't that why they get to charge you $142,000? Why are you paying for *their* business costs? (Hint: because we let them get away with it.)

The same goes for title insurance. In most cases you'll need title insurance. That can set you back $1,000 or more. The mortgage company requires this, but guess who pays for it?

You'll start getting a better idea of the nature of these fees if you spend a bit of time online at consumer advocate websites. Most will tell you that such closing costs are "negotiable."

Those of us who have ventured out into the world understand that the phrase "negotiable costs" is often a synonym for "scam." Any cost or fee that's "negotiable" is likely something someone made up to see if you'd pay it. Either it costs $500 to print out some forms or it doesn't.

Why does the buyer pay for surveys the finance company requests and charges for? And credit report fees for their assessment of your credit. And processing fees to cover the cost of creating that pile of documents for you to sign.

Again, doesn't this sound like their daily overhead costs? The cost of making money merely for lending it out should include finding out if people are credit worthy, checking the property lines, and printing forms to sign. Right?

Usury used to be illegal. Many might think 75% to 120% interest

Well, Ms. House Buyer. We've never had such a wild and crazy request before but we somehow managed to print out these forms for you to sign. Of course, it will cost you.

qualifies. If the mortgage lenders are going to pursue usury professionally you'd think they'd at least do the paperwork for you. Apparently not.

Predictably, the government has its hand out at closing time as well. For the most part, government costs like recording fees and taxes are not negotiable. Not because they aren't ludicrous, but because the government doesn't have to negotiate with you, Citizen.

Right or wrong, fair or criminal, if you decide to buy a house you'll be writing checks for all of this. Unless….

Unless you can negotiate some of it away. Even if you decide to ignore 99.93% of the advice in this book and buy a house with conventional mortgage financing (you fool!), at least take the time to check the consumer websites and try their "Negotiate Closing Costs" tips.

These tips change over time. Due to the made-up, whatever-they-can-get-away with nature of closing costs, the best advice for negotiation can vary. So we can't give you a definitive list. Check online.

We've found examples of buyer's closing costs that equal 7.5% of house value. That would be $15,000 for our hypothetical $200,000 house. We've also found buyer's closing costs in the 1% range. That would equal $2,000 for our example. These are atypical extremes. Online house-pushers Zillow estimate closing costs between 2% and 5% of value. Our modest and conservative estimate for a typical buyer's closing costs for a $200,000 house would be 3% ($6,000).

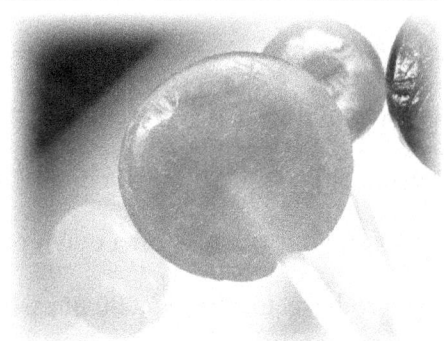

A willingness to pay all these fees reminds us of a certain confection.

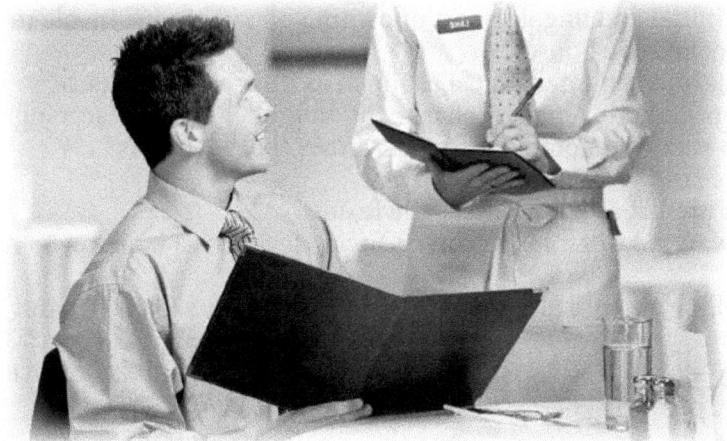

I'll take $140,000 in effortless profit and give the bill to that guy over there.

What are a typical seller's closing costs? <u>Money</u> magazine says 5% to 8% of value. Realtor.com says 6% to 10%. We've found that 8% is a good general estimate. Especially when you understand that the real estate broker's fees alone are typically between 6% and 7%. For our $200,000 house the real estate fee alone will be $12,000 to $14,000.

Our conservative estimate for seller's closing costs will be 8% of $200,000, or $16,000.

Closing Costs

As you might have noticed if you were paying attention a moment ago, a house owner really pays closing costs two times! Yes! When they buy and then again when they sell. Sellers pay the bulk of the costs. But buyers pay too. If you buy a house, then later sell it, you'll pay both. But what if you the buyer have already spent all your pennies on a down payment, buying out your lease, hiring movers, and some vodka? Now you need to have another $6,000 in cash at closing?

Ah. Not to worry. Our new friends at the mortgage finance corporation want to help! They will allow you the buyer to "fold in" the buyers closing costs to the price of the house. You can just add this $6,000 to your principle. And pay interest on it. For 30 years.

Your $6,000 will then cost you $19,460.39. Plus you'll pay the seller's closing costs when you finally bail out. Seller's costs of $16,000.

So the total transaction bill for coming, and for going, through the world of house ownership totals $35,460.

Mortgage:	$342,456
PMI:	$ 14,100
Taxes	$ 75,000
Insurance	$ 45,000
Repair & Replace	$150,000
~~Luxury extras~~	~~$ 60,000~~ $0 (Not counted)
Upgrades	$ 60,000
2nd Mortgage	$ 41,460
Closing costs	$ 35,460
Cost of $200,000 house:	$763,484 (so far)

Chapter 2 take-aways:
- To simply finance a $200,000 house in the very average circumstances we outline you will actually pay $342,000. Just for the financing.
- The house pushers vastly underestimate the initial and ongoing cost of owning a house, presumable in order to convince more people to buy more expensive houses.
- Taxes and insurance are very substantial costs and can total almost as much as financing the house.
- The costs left out of "affordability" calculations include repair, replacement, upgrades and landscaping which (according to the experts that sell this stuff) can total four to eight times the ridiculous "1%" figure the industry use, far exceeding the price of the house over 30 years.
- The outside of your house is feral, needy and almost as expensive as the inside.
- Second mortgages are very common and one of the worst long term financial decisions a house owner can make.
- The transaction costs for buying and then selling a house are formidable, adding up to $35,000 for our example house.
- The out-of-pocket costs of financing and owning a house can be expected to exceed the purchase price by four to six times over 30 years.

Chapter 3: Where are the Profits?

Just as with the discussion of house costs, the standard discussion of house profits departs immediately from the true, sane and comprehensible.

One example: Houses are supposed to "appreciate." That means they should be worth more tomorrow than they were yesterday. In general, over time, in many places, that's somewhat true. Kinda-sorta. But not always.

Even when they do appreciate, however, houses don't appreciate for the same reason or at the same rate that an successful investment like a corporate stock, or a Picasso appreciates. Houses are just consumer products. They deteriorate, go out of style, and often lose value.

Let's repeat that for emphasis and so that the book reviewers will have a great quote:

--Houses often *lose* value--

When houses do go up in price it is largely because of inflation. Let's briefly discuss inflation. Inflation means that each year stuff in general costs a bit more than it did before.[36] Sometimes—as it did during an extreme period in the 1970s and 1980s—inflation goes crazy and consumer goods start increasing in price at a dizzying rate. A house that cost $20,000 in 1971 might have cost $30,000 in 1975. Not because houses are awesome money-creating machines, but because the cost of everything went up by that much: cars; chairs; eight-track tape players; Partridge-Family-themed lunch boxes. (Just one more reason the 1970s sucked.)

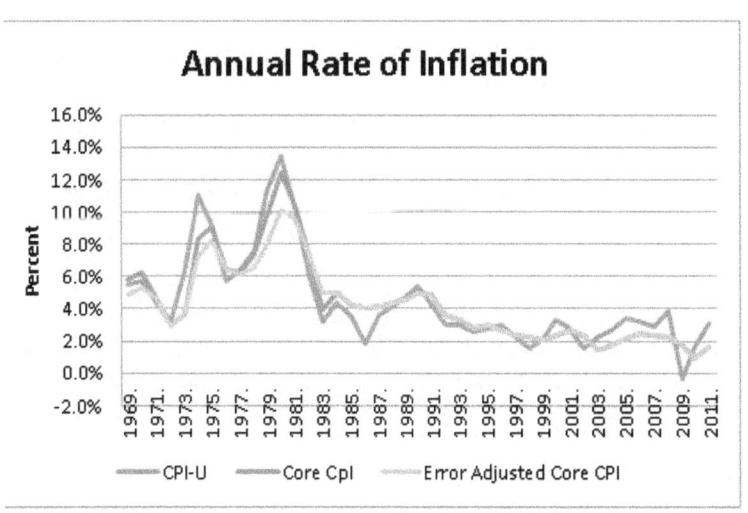

Keep that in mind when older folks who bought houses in the 1960s and 1970s tell you how much money they "made" with their houses. All they did was watch the numbers move like a cheap magic trick. If everything

---

36 There is also a phenomenon known as deflation where everything loses value. We've been spared that, so far, in the USA so we needn't discuss it here.

Chapter 3: Where are the Profits

costs twice as much, then you've gained nothing just because your house has doubled in price, too. In fact, economists tell us that houses actually *lost* value as the prices of everything skyrocketed during the 1970s.[37]

Why is inflation so important? Don't houses go up in price in addition to inflation? Not usually. Certainly not enough to offset the cost of having one. Certainly not enough to bet your financial future on.

According to our friends at the National Association for Realtors®, on average the price of existing homes increased by 5.4% annually from 1968 to 2009.[38] The Census Bureau reports the same figure for new homes for a similar period. Adjusting for the fact that average houses grew much bigger over time and so comparing averages isn't an accurate yard stick, that annual rate of appreciation is 3.7%. Inflation during that time averaged 4.5%. So even using NAR's numbers, *similar houses during the past 40 years didn't even appreciate as fast as inflation. That means they lost value.*

Even the hard-nosed, corporate Capitalist cheerleading pro-house Wall Street Journal[39] will grudgingly admit that—adjusted for inflation—similar sized houses with similar amenities have *dropped* in value since 1978.

"Nobel Laureate Dr. Robert Shiller's research revealed that house values have only gone up an average of 0.2% a year over the past 100 years."

But the real kicker is research conducted by Yale economist, Nobel Laureate, and America's "foremost expert on house values," Dr. Robert Shiller. Dr. Shiller discovered that house values have only gone up an average of 0.2% a year over the past 100 years. Not the ridiculous 4% to 6% or even 8% house pushers claim.[40]

Huh? What the hell?? That is very bizarre. Why haven't we heard of these numbers? Maybe because there is no large lobbying group with half a trillion dollars to spend that wants to publicize such research?

The interesting part is that the financial insiders know about this research. They know the real numbers.

---

37 Certain people suspect that such inflationary periods are purposefully moved by the economically powerful to "squeeze" all the value out of the economy, enriching themselves. Such people point out the cyclical nature of these "crises." And how income inequality tends to change drastically. And how inflation confuses us average folks so we don't know we are getting fleeced. But—of course—that is just crazy talk.

38 (NAR Real Estate ABC, p.1, p.2).

39 http://blogs.wsj.com/economics/2015/04/28/why-new-homes-have-become-more-expensive-theyre-much-bigger/

40 (See also, Irrational Exuberance). According to Census records, in 1915 a typical house would cost about $3,200. Whoa! Sounds like houses have made big gains. However, while median income is in 2015 is $53,046, in 1915 average income was only $687 a year. Even a $3,200 house is tough to afford if you only make $687 a year. 1915 house owners also had coal bills to pay and horseless carriages to maintain, you know.

Chapter 3: Where are the Profits

Of course they do. Financiers count on research like this to make sure *their* wealth is secure.

This information isn't hidden. It's not a secret. Dr. Shiller writes books. He is a Nobel Laureate, remember? Yale University? Occasionally the WSJ or Forbes or Zillow or the NAR screws up and publicizes a bit of it while trying to make another related point. So this information is out there people if want to find it. But they don't, apparently. Maybe most people never look for that sort of sound, professional, economic research because (for some reason) we are all already convinced we know the answer; we know that houses are our path to long-term wealth and security even if they are not.

But wait. Maybe the point is still a bit confusing. What is all this "adjusting for inflation" stuff? Call it what you will, if the house goes up in price isn't the owner making money? No. Not if it isn't going up in price faster than everything else.

Let's look at this inflation idea from another angle. Let's look at value rather than dollars.

If that $20,000 house bought in 1971 is equal in value to 40,000 Partridge Family lunch boxes, then it's worth approximately the same 40,000 lunch boxes in 1975 at $30,000. The house and the lunch boxes have not really increased in value. Yes, both the house and lunch boxes cost more. But only because the money itself has lost value.

When money loses value you need more of it to keep score. Across the board.

This sort of rising price is not the same thing as the increase in value that comes from a good investment. Inflation just results in everyone moving wheelbarrow-loads of money around in order to buy lunch. Inflation doesn't make money for consumers.

Seems like only yesterday when we needed a mere half wheelbarrow of money to buy a latte!

More bad news. Not only do inflation-driven price increases fail to benefit house owners, when inflation is low—as in the current market—housing prices tend to stagnate or drop. So while other investments are making profits, money tied up in houses just sits and grows mold.

Some even worse news. When the bottom falls out of the housing market—as it did in 2008—almost every person in the country who owns a house suddenly loses money.

Chapter 3: Where are the Profits

The average house lost 25% of its value when the market crashed. Some lost 50% of their value. Most have never fully recovered. If you had bought our example house for $200,000 in 2007 it would now be worth about $155,000. U.S. houses lost $6 trillion dollars ($6,000,000,000,000) during that crash. Yowzer.

Real investments, on the other hand, like a Picasso, should increase in value at a rate many times that of inflation. Much more rapidly than the price of houses. In fact, good investments tend to be more valuable in a bad economy because people use them as a refuge to protect wealth against inflation and other economic ills.

True appreciation does sometimes happen to houses. It's rare, but possible. You might make money, for example, if your house is located in an area that suddenly becomes a boomtown, overrun by people who want to live there badly enough to pay $300,000 for the exact house you bought for $200,000 two years ago. Think San Fransisco, Boston, Brooklyn, Washington D.C. and other trendy cities during certain periods.

Detroit houses like this one didn't just grow there, you know. Some poor fool paid full price, plus interest, taxes, insurance and upkeep for this place. 1,999,999, other Detroiters did the same. Tens of millions of people in Cleveland, Flint, Pittsburgh, New Orleans, Philly, Toledo, St. Louis, Buffalo, parts of L.A and NYC, and other formerly "cool cities" did the same. *Memento, homo quia pulvis es, et in pulverem reverteris.* That's Latin for "someday your neighborhood will be a slum, too."

That's pretty good news for the house seller in such a market. Can you see why it might not be such a great deal in the long run for the buyer? The buyer is betting that this irrational spike in prices becomes permanent. Ask people who bought houses in Las Vegas during its recent boom (spoiler: that boom was followed by a crash) how that worked out for them.

This sort of boomtown house appreciation isn't a rule. It's unlikely and unpredictable and not the basis for sound investment strategy. You just plain cannot count on houses to appreciate.

In fact, sometimes the opposite happens. Sometimes houses depreciate. Yes!

You won't hear much about this from the house pushers. While they like to spotlight people who bought houses at the right time in boomtowns and enjoyed rapid increases in value, they rarely mention what happened to the people who bought those overpriced houses in Vegas. Or to the two million people who owned houses in Detroit in the 1950s, or house owners in Pittsburgh. Or Cleveland or Philadelphia or Baltimore or Flint or the Bronx or St. Louis or dozens of other formerly booming cities that were "sure bets" in their day.

Tens of millions of average, hardworking people just like you people bought houses that ended up being worth little or nothing when it came time to sell them.

Myth Versus Reality.

Recall that one of the main themes of this book is that most of the elements that support the pro-house argument are myths, lies and nonsense.

Like the beliefs of a cult, you're expected to accept—not question—these pro-house axioms:

- Your house will magically increase in value, even if it doesn't.
- Your endless infusions of additional cash will increase the value of your house, even if they don't.
- The mere potential to deduct some small percentage of the tens of thousands of dollars you spend in interest on your mortgage, in some circumstances, will cancel out the fact that you had to spend all those tens of thousands in mortgage interest and much more, even if that isn't so.
- The cost of borrowing all that money, and spending and tying up much more money over time, will be less than the profit you'll make, even if it isn't.
- The Bhagwahn is both the light and the dark, the sky and the earth, and his fleet of Rolls Royces are the embodiment of a pure, non-materialistic life, even if they aren't. (Wait. Sorry, wrong cult.)

This book is incapable of holding such ridiculous views and still maintaining a healthy level of self-esteem. So, again, this book presents another simple rule. This one regarding profits. Simple rule:

If you make money from owning a house

that you'd not have made otherwise, it's profit.

Mortgage Interest Deductions
(Paying $20 for a $5 bill)

In the nascent stages of drafting this book there was extensive research conducted on the tax benefits of house ownership.[41] Our goal from the outset was to be fair and to give the other side—the house pushers—a fair shake, which is more than they usually do for us poor schmucks who buy houses.

There are no Cinderella Stories in house buying.

Mostly we wanted to make sure we didn't leave any easy mistakes they could use to attack the entire book. *"See how on page 86 they claim that a house will ruin your life in only a year? See that!?! It can actually take as long as two years for a house to ruin your life! Obviously the book is wrong and we're right. Therefore, buy a house!"*

So we expressed these fairness concerns to our CPA/tax guru. There's a need to be very careful, we said. Give the house-pushers the benefit of the doubt, we added. Fairly express their perspective. Take a fair and balanced look at their math.

Given these goals, we asked the CPA: what are the many tax benefits of owning a house?

In many ways his reply summarizes the wisdom and overall perspective of this book.

He said, "Huh? What benefits?"

~~Further drinking~~ ... further research revealed that there are really only two income tax "benefits" from buying a single-family house and they are both more BS than substance. First, you get to deduct mortgage interest. Second, in some situations, there's a deduction for state property taxes. That's it.

It's also worth noting here the tax guru's response to our questions about the pervasive myth of house ownership as investment: *"It's bullshit. The whole thing is bullshit. Most people lose big on houses. About the best you can hope for is to keep your head above water for 30 years. Then maybe your kids could inherit it. They don't know all the money you wasted on it. They don't give a shit."*

Doesn't this photo of a tax form and money lend our inebriated ponderings an aura of authenticity?

---

41 AKA: We sat and drank a beer with a buddy who is a CPA and professional tax expert

Mortgage Interest Deductions

To break down the tax implications of financing a house let's recall the many lessons we've learned so far while tallying up the costs of our example house. This hypothetical house cost $200,000 and was financed for 30 years using a conventional mortgage at 4.5%. So the final cost of principle and interest at the end of 30 years was $342,456.

In the beginning, interest is all. You pay almost nothing on the principle. The principle is the money you owe on your house, not including interest. So all your money, month after month, is going almost entirely toward paying tens of thousands of dollars in interest (and taxes and PMI and insurance and repairs). In other words, you're paying your bank its profit up front before you ever start paying off the house.

So if you pay and pay and pay for a few years and then through some miracle of medical science you regain your sanity and decide to ditch the house, you might find you spent tens of thousands of dollars and still owe as much as when you started. But at least you get all that interest back on your taxes. Right?

Well....no. No you don't.

If you meet some qualifications (and only about one-third of taxpayers do) you may qualify for a Mortgage Interest Deduction. (MID).[42] Even if you qualify, all this means is that you can deduct mortgage interest you paid from your total taxable income so you don't pay taxes on that amount a second time. You *don't* get all that interest refunded to you. You *don't* get all that money back.

An easy rule of thumb is that you only benefit about one-quarter to one-third of the mortgage interest you pay. The rest? Gone with the wind.

So how do the house-pushers figure the MID is a boast-worthy "benefit" of owning a house? Right out of the gate, two-thirds of people don't qualify. Even for those who qualify, if they didn't own a house they wouldn't have paid *any* mortgage interest at all. A non-house owner would have *all* that money in their pocket. So the small remainder of your money you might receive on a tax return because of the MID, again, isn't so much a profit you made as a loss you were able to minimize (to some degree).

If your fiancé dumped you for a neighbor and ran off with your dog and your pickup truck and your granddad's red, white and blue rifle, but gave you a kiss on the way out the door, is

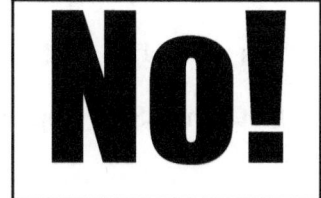

---

[42] We are not tax experts. We are not giving you professional advice. We are writing a funny book. Go ask your own tax expert.

that kiss a benefit you gained?

(Hint: No.)

Similarly, any MID for which you might qualify is a kind of subtle kiss-off: "Give me your dollars and I'll toss you back some change. Maybe."

However, to be fair in our example, we do need to count deductions like the MID and track how they minimize the total amount of pain you experiencing with your house. The MID does help (slightly) to reduce your losses.

If you qualify. Whether you qualify for an MID depends on your income.

(Warning: small amounts of math.) Financial advisers tell us that housing costs should not exceed 30% of gross income. So to afford a $200,000 house, household income needs to be at least $58,000.

That puts a qualified buyer in the 15% tax bracket. An average taxpayer in the 15% bracket will receive a $2383.61 MID-related refund. If the taxpayer qualifies. However, few taxpayers with a $58,000 gross income will have the $12,000 in itemized deductions necessary to qualify.[43]

So, for our $200,000 example, it's possible that even less than one-third of taxpayers would qualify.

But, hey, let's follow the house-pushing bullshit to the end of the trail. Say that our house buyer example does qualify. What does that mean? It means that in our example the bank takes $8,934 in Mortgage Interest, and Uncle Sam sends you back $2,300.

Let's harken back to 1st grade and do some arithmetic.

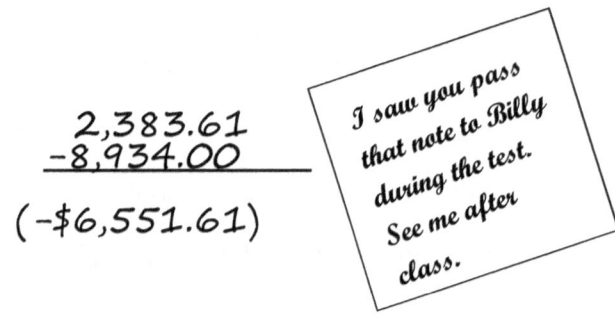

This is your promised MID "profit??"

It is a $6551.61 *loss*. So far. This year. Just in interest.

Hot damn. Slow clap. We are rolling in the house-profit Benjamins now.

---

43 Source, the IRS.

You could be an MID Fat Cat!

Again, almost all the money you pay in mortgage each month goes toward interest for the first few years. Over time, the amount you pay in interest gradually decreases until, in the last few years of your 30 year mortgage, principle makes up most of your payments.

So that means the MID is much more "valuable" during the first half of the 30-year life of a mortgage. Just when financial advisors say most people have the lowest incomes and are therefore less likely to qualify for the MID. When you can use it, you can't have it. When you can get it, you don't need it. And even when you can have it and can get it, it is really an overall loss.

In other words, things in MID land start out bad and just keep getting worse as time goes by.

What do you think it means that the house pushers roll out this lame bit of BS as one of their better "pro-house" talking points?

Property Tax Deduction

The other tax "benefit" our crafty tax guru uncovered is a house owner's ability to deduct the property taxes paid the previous year from this year's taxes. This is the "Property Tax Deduction" (PTD).

If you didn't have a house you'd pay $0.00 in property taxes. That seems to be the best possible position. Doesn't it? If you buy a house, on the other hand, you do have to pay property taxes.

Recall that our $200,000 house comes with an average tax bill of $2500. This means that our house owner will pay about $75,000 over thirty years. As opposed to no property taxes.

And the big PTD benefit? Each year the IRS won't charge income taxes on the property taxes paid the year before. Isn't that thoughtful of them?

You *don't* get your $2,500 back. We can't say that enough. For some reason many people assume that's what happens. They pay $2500 in property taxes, but Uncle Sam just sends it back to them.

No.

Instead, the IRS subtracts $2,500 from your total taxable income. So you don't get taxed on that $2,500. If you made $50,000 this year, for example, with a PTD the IRS deals with you as if you made $47,500.

What the hell does that mean for your bank account? If you're like 99% of taxpayers your tax "benefit" will be approximately one-quarter to one-third of property taxes you paid. So by paying $2500 in extra taxes, you'll "benefit" by getting back—roughly—between $750 and $825.

The higher the amount you get back through PTD the better for the pro-house argument, so let's be magnanimous and assume $800 per year as our example PTD benefit. It makes the math easy and can help counter some of their inevitable objections: again we've given up some ground.

Again, just as with the MID, this $800 PTD isn't a "benefit" in any way.

Both PTD and MID are really just ways to slow the flood of lost income.

House owning profits so far.

PTD	$ 800
Cost:	-$2500
"Benefit"	-$1700 (loss)

Wow. The money is ~~just rolling in~~ . . . rolling out at a slightly reduced rate. Notify the media.

Remember, dear reader, that the MID and PTD deductions aren't our strawmen[44] defense of financing a house. These two arguments are rolled out by the house pushers and their shills as examples. This is one of their supporting arguments.

Speaking of "strawmen."

The Strawmen: Landlords

A strange, but surprisingly strong and widespread, pro-house argument is the mere existence of landlords.

The pro-house reasoning goes like this: if landlords can rent me a house and still make money, it must be cheaper to buy a house myself, right?

Not so fast there, Socrates.[45]

You're standing on a huge pile of unexamined assumptions. Let's help

Is it odd that this scary character represents landlords rather than money-for-nothing house

---

44 A "strawman" argument is a purposely weak argument that is easily countered, rolled out by the opposing side as the main argument against them—then defeated—to "prove" the othe side is wrong.

45 "So-crates:" famous philosopher from ancient Greece, best known for his minor role in the 1989 film, Bill & Ted's Excellent Adventure.

you down before you get hurt.

Here are some facts for you consider:

Many landlords don't have mortgages. They own their rentals free and clear, having paid for them outright. They own properties with no mortgage interest, no PMI, and none of those other third-party-profit costs that are kicking your butt if you own a house. So they can afford to rent for a lot less than you can buy. Other landlords have large properties, or a great many properties, and therefore the banks treat them with a kindness and understanding you'll never experience in terms of advantageous financing terms.

Landlords also don't spend money on frivolous extras like upholstered ceilings, indoor waterfalls and heated garage floors. They buy simple but heavy-duty components that last. They buy at serious discounts, or used, or recycled. To them, a house isn't a place to show off or indulge: it's a business.

(If you do go and buy a house, keep that strategy in mind.)

Even with this business mentality in place, many landlords don't have a positive cash flow. That means they lose money each month by renting to you for less than their costs. Why would they do that? There are many possible reasons for keeping a house and renting it at a loss. Maybe, like the house owner in our next example, a landlord is sitting on a house that's underwater. Maybe they figure they'll ride out the market for a few years and take a $200 a month loss rather than face a $50,000 immediate loss if they sell the place.

Other people who are losing money to rent to you might want to keep a house in a particular area for some personal reason. Maybe it's the house they grew up in, or they plan to retire there someday. Maybe they have a kid who will be attending college nearby and they want to hang on to the house until their college student grows up. Maybe they're at year 28 of a 30-year mortgage and are just trying to get the place paid off.

Some landlords lose money each month, but hope that in the long run they will build equity. That's actually possible if interest payments from two mortgages, a tendency to buy posh extras and PMI payments aren't sucking up all the money.

Maybe your landlord is the guardian of an elderly couple who are in nursing care. The couple wants to

---

My favorite neighbor: *"He names all the squirrels in the neighborhood and closely tracks their movements. After he came by my house one day asking if he could climb a tree in my front yard to rescue a nest of baby squirrels whose mom had been run over, I realized that the "lower the speed limit" petition he'd taken door to door last year was out of concern for the squirrels and not the kids in the neighborhood. Nice guy, though."*

keep their house, bless their hearts, because they assume they will "get better" someday and move back in. Renters are getting a good deal on rent until the kids inherit it.

> "Buying a house because you need a place to live is like buying a restaurant because you need something to eat."
> - Jack Sheppard

Maybe your landlord is just bad with accounting, like most house owners. Maybe lots of things. Life is strange. People are even stranger. If you can save some bucks because someone else is willing to rent you a house for $1,600 a month that would cost you the equivalent of $2050 per month in payments, insurance, repairs, forgone income, and taxes to buy, their reasons (from your financial perspective) don't matter much.[46]

What you should not do is assume that because someone is renting you a house for $1,600 per month you'd be ahead of the game by just buying it yourself. Maybe you're right, but likely, you aren't.[47]

"Ya' Gotta Live Somewhere" (Replacing Rent)

Of all the arguments with the apparent potential to tip the balance in favor of owning a house, there's one that might be the MVP. Here is it: You have to live somewhere, right? So why not buy a house so that your money is creating equity. Right?

Almost everyone has heard this lame cliché and most people will drag it out of storage if you suggest that buying a house might not be the best idea. "Well, after all," they'll say, often adopting a mindless drawl, "ya gotta live somewhere!"

Broken down, this is the argument: since you must pay for a place to live, why not be paying for a house and get some of your money back rather than be paying rent and tossing all of your money away?

Though almost everyone in the house debate mentions this reasoning, almost no one gets it right.

Here is the flaw. People who make this argu-

> "I rented versus bought for years while I saved up to pay cash for my house. People told me I was mad but the point was. 1)I was renting a basic place below the standard I would buy, and 2)All the extra coin I saved went into investments and worked for me compounding. All the rubbish about borrowing money and paying off house just didn't add up on paper. When I crunched the numbers it didn't work. Paying fees and interest on home loan left me in debt versus the 10 percent I got investing. Worked for me. Just do the numbers for your personal situation, don't believe people that are neck deep in debt, usually they are just continuing the pitch the bank gave them".

---

46 We spoke with landlords in each one of these situations.

47 No. You would be wrong.

ment (incorrectly) assume that renting and buying cost about the same amount, or, that buying is cheaper than renting. If you are going to pay a dollar for rent or a dollar for house financing, they posit, at least you might get back a penny from your house financing dollar, right? A penny is better than nothing.

But what if house owners pay *more* for owning a house than they would have paid in rent? Significantly more. Way more than that hypothetical "penny" in profit? Like we have proven in exhausting detail over the past few dozen pages?

Here is one of the most important and most surprising facts in this book. So we will shamelessly use bold face, italics and underlining all in one sentence: We are even going to change font!

In most cases <u>houses cost *much* more to finance and keep up than to rent</u>. In most cases <u>houses cost more than any possible equity a house owner could build in them</u>.

Let's look at an example. Let's say you can rent a place to live that's very much like our $200,000 house for $1,600 per month. Now, the house pushers will tell you that the $200,000 house only costs $1,120 per month so buying is a clean winner.

Ha! Not so fast.

When we factor in all of the actual costs we've been discussing (that our pro-house friends leave out) the actual out-of-pocket cost for buying and upkeep on that $200,000 house (not just the financing) are at least $2050 per month.

Because houses cost so much more than the conventional wisdom says, it is the renters who win big. The renters in our example run off with an extra $450 per month.

Recall that in order for the "gotta live somewhere" argument to hold water, a house buyer would need to be socking away more equity than the premium they're paying to buy. In this case a house buyer would need to be accumulating $450 per month in equity just to break even with the renter. In addition, at the break-even point a house owner is still doing all the work and taking on the headaches of house ownership, and all that just to break even.

Renter running off with saved money!

Let's not forget those burdens, responsibility and risk a house owner is taking on. That has value and cost.

So in order to really justify the argument a house buyer would need to be accumulating *more* than $450 per month in equity. That's over $5400 a year. If you remember our ongoing accounting, our hypothetical house was *losing* a lot more than that each year, not making it.

> Here is another cost of owning a house we didn't even count: the so-called "utility premium." According to the folks who measure utility usage, house owners use up to *double* the electricity, gas and water renters use.

Wait. That's just the beginning. Since we're all pretending to be fiscally responsible adults here, and not typical American consumers, we're going to put that $450 per month rent savings to work for us. We're going to invest it.

It really doesn't matter where we invest the money. It's almost impossible to find a rate of return less than the appreciation of home values. Bonds? Savings account? Partridge Family lunch boxes on ebay? All fine.

As long as we don't loan it to my brother-in-law who believes he has solved the mystery of perpetual motion, earnings on that monthly $450 investment, times 360 months, will far outpace any earnings we're likely to gain by "building equity" in a house. Say we earn a conservative 3% on the $450 we invest every month. Let's use the mighty power of compound interest to see where that leaves us after 30 years.

Shazaam! We've just earned $263,992. Better than that, we turned $162,000 ($450 x 12 x 30) in unspent house owning costs into $263,992 and we did it by making our lives easier and reducing our work, frustration and problems by not financing a house!

This large forgone sum, $263,992, is the opportunity cost of tying up money in a house. This is money a house buyer could have earned, but gave up to buy into some dandelions and caulk. Pro-house financing folks generally don't bother to mention this cost.

Know why?

Because if house pushers considered the higher costs of buying, and the opportunity cost of paying that extra, then their house =

> Let's stop playing softball with the house-pushers for a minute. By now you should be ready to see past the myths and digest some sobering facts. If we look at the cumulative total of our estimates from financing and taxes to upkeep and opportunity cost we discover that $200,000 house is likely to cost well over $1,000,000 and could conceivably cost more than $2,100,000 over 30 years. THAT, dear reader, is the magnitude of the scheme we are dissecting here. We are talking about throwing away the benefits of a lifetime of working. How much do you want a house?

value math doesn't work.

We aren't done yet. Imagine if we did something even better with that $450 per month. Let's say we're semi-savvy investors. Say we could earn 4% on our investment. Now we have created $314,854.

But that's still weak. This is someone's future we're talking about here. Let's do our hypothetical person a solid and find an even better home for that $450 monthly savings.

Financial advisors tell us that investing on Wall Street could bring us long term returns in the range of 8% to 10%.

Holy comfortable retirement, Batman! $450 per month at 8% over 30 years would earn $675,582! If we believe the Wall Street folks (and I'm not saying we should) that same $450 per month over 30 years at 10% would end up creating a very impressive $1,026,146.

But let's stick with our conservative and realistic 4% ROI for our example. That equals $314,854 a house owner would give up in opportunity costs. Back to our running cost total:

Mortgage:	$ 342,456	
PMI:	$ 14,100	
Taxes	$ 75,000	
Insurance	$ 45,000	
Repair & Replace	$ 150,000	
~~Luxury extras~~	~~$ 60,000~~	$0 (Not counted)
Upgrades	$ 60,000	
2nd Mortgage	$ 41,460	
Closing costs	$ 35,460	
Opportunity cost	$ 314,854	
Cost of $200,000 house:	$ 1,078,338 (not including $105,000 in additional costs)	

Even using our modest, conservative numbers that "$200,000 house" is going to cost over ... one MIL-LION dollars. [Pinkie to mouth, Dr. Evil style.]

"Wait a minute," the house-pushers exclaim, "even if all that stuff you claim about houses costing a fortune, and house owners spending all their spare change on heated driveways and S&M dungeons is true—and we say it isn't—you're leaving out a very important consideration!"

Aha! The house pushers have one last card up their sleeves. (Cue ominous music.)

Much better! Last time they hid a three of clubs.

The "Locked-In Payment" Argument

If you dig long enough through the inky goo of pro-house rhetoric you'll always find this nugget of pseudo-truth: the "locked-in payment" argument.

Here's how they explain it. Buying a house "locks in" your monthly payment. If you're paying $2050 per month now, you'll still be paying $2050 per month in 30 years. Rent, on the other hand, might have possibly doubled or tripled by then.

Before we become "locked in" maybe we should take a look at what we are being locked in to?

"Aha," the house-pushers announce with glee, not understanding the concept of subtlety at all, "we did it! We finally proved that houses are a great deal!!"

Au contraire, proxénètes maison.[48]

Let's pause and appreciate this moment. We aren't only staring at a single particularly bad argument. Here we've uncovered one of the fatal flaws behind every house buying argument.

Pro-house arguments in general and this one in particular, assume our house owner will be sitting in that one house for 30 years.

Guess what? Americans don't do that. We move. Many of us move a lot. In fact, almost all of us do. The Census Bureau and the moving industry tell us at least 11.5% of American move each year. That means, on average, that each of us moves at least every nine years or so. So, during the time we're supposedly sitting in our houses, not going to the Grand Canyon, not buying a new laptop, putting our money into HOA fees and cement counter tops, we have actually moved. At least three times.

Three times the cost and misery!

And guess what happens each time we Americans move? We sell our houses. And we buy others. So we *triple* our transactions costs. Three times the transaction fees Gail® uses to send our Congresscritters to Bermuda; three times the BS closing costs; three times the almost-inter-

---

48 That means "Not quite, honored house-pushing sir!" in Klingon. (Just kidding. It's actually Mandarin for "Oh no you di'int!)"

est-only monthly payments, three times all those other large and compounding expenses.

But that isn't even the rim shot.

Each time we move and pay Gail®, pay closing costs, pay 75% interest and PMI and renovation and upgrade costs and taxes, our monthly payments go up. Of course they do. Because that inflation-driven value appreciation we were told would help us build easy wealth is now kicking us while we're down.

How? Well, when we sell the $200,000 house after nine years we expect to sell for more than $200,000 thanks to inflation. So when we look for a replacement house, guess what? The new but similar house will cost more, too. That means even bigger payments. Plus, you know, our taxes and insurance and repair and upkeep costs have gone up, thanks to inflation, right along with any "appreciation" the house might experience. Those expenses—the big ones—are not locked in.

So there goes the house-pusher argument about "locking in payments." Doesn't work like that in the real world. Like renting, house owning costs will go up each time we relocate.

Each time we sell before the 30 year mortgage is up we take a hit because most of the money hasn't been going to pay off the house; we've mostly been paying all that interest, fees, taxes, and insurance. Little of our money has been going to principle and equity. We've been making big monthly mortgage payments, but the money is being siphoned off into other people's pockets.

At our nine-year moving-mark, we're not building equity comparable with our out of pocket costs or a renter's savings. We're still just spending money, a lot more money than the renters.

Even after 20 years of monthly payments and repairs and taxes and insurance, etc., we still haven't even paid off half the original cost of the house.

If we sell in the first five or six years of the mortgage? Even *les proxénètes maison*[49] will admit that we would take a nasty cold financial bath in that case. After five years a house owner has paid off almost none of the principle, but has been paying taxes, insurance and upkeep that are significantly higher than rent, and will be handing Gail® another big check.

Then, again, all over with the next house. Rinse and repeat.

---

49 An old Navajo phrase meaning "wise financial mentor."

Our friends the renters, on the other hand, are still building up their $314,854 from investing the money they save by not buying. (Or if they continue to show the smarts that led them to avoid financing a house, they might be investing toward that $1,026,146!)

When the renters move—as most of us do—all they will have to do is give notice, scrounge some boxes off of Craigslist®, and head out of or across town. They'll need to put down a security deposit for their new rental, and might incur some other minor expenses, but they should be able to cover those costs with the security deposit returned to them from their last place.

They're also in no danger of yet another scary house-buying trap: having to make mortgage payments on a house that won't sell while also standing the expense of a new house. The dreaded "double mortgage." Not a concern for our renters.

As we have explored and demonstrated, about 60% of the cost of a financed house over 30 years isn't the allegedly locked in mortgage. The really big costs relate to the obligations, repair and upkeep of houses, and the opportunity cost of tying up all that money. And those costs are not locked in.

Rents Increase?

The myth of "locked in" payments working to your benefit has a drinking buddy: the notion that rents always increase.

But what if rents don't always increase?

Over the past half-century both property values and rents have declined in many places, and at many different times. One of these declines occurred during the 2008 mortgage heist. They've occurred in many boom-and-bust places like Las Vegas. In almost every city in the rust belt. In areas that have experienced natural disasters. In markets that face regional economic woes. In cities and neighborhoods that are no longer fashionable.

What happens to renters and buyers in such a situation? Here sits our house owner, comfortable and satisfied with a "locked-in" monthly house payment while across the road Those Foolish Renters are foolishly paying (less) for their similar rental place.

Suddenly: Boom! Housing values and prices drop. Maybe a factory closes or a school gets shot up or a hurricane hits or a commodity price like oil or corn drops. Who knows what the hammer blow will be? Life is fragile, grasshopper, and the only constant is change.

In this falling housing market our house owner is paying "locked in" mortgage payments plus house owning penalties, and suffering the opportunity costs of putting money into crabgrass instead of real investments. Meanwhile, the renting neighbors face one of two possible futures. Either their rent payments will drop or they will move down the street to a place with cheaper rent.

And the house buyer? Stuck like a rat in a trap. "Locked in" we might say. No one wants to buy that house now. It's "underwater;" that is, the owner owes more on the house than it would sell for in the current market, even if someone wanted it. But they don't.

Each month the house owner loses more and more money. Any hope of ever making a profit is gone; the house owners just wants to cut losses. How? What options are there?

Obviously a house owner facing such a situation is going to cancel the new bathroom remodel. Maybe return that tiki bar to the big box store. In a few years, if they're lucky, the local government might knock back a couple of bucks on property taxes.

But most of a house owner's expenses are carrying costs that are out of their control. Remember? Our house owner has "locked-in" all these costs, persuaded by the house-financing lobby and their fairy tales about infinite increasing house values.

And that is the no-win situation that tens of millions of Americans have faced during the past few decades, one that Gail® and her ilk never talk about: being "locked-in" to a sinking ship house.

House Tally: So Much for "Profit"

Let's not ruin all the house buying fun by being too focused on facts and realistic possibilities. Just for a moment, we'll paint a more cheerful picture for you, the potential house buyer.

Let's assume you qualified and received your maximum MID and PTD credits. Let's assume no recent Wall Street "crises" or "crashes" and that your neighborhood contains no crazy cat-poisoners or window-shooters. Let's assume that you've stuck it out at in your house for a full 30 years. Let's assume that your repair costs in that time were less than half of what the manufacturers and service people predict, and that you spent less than half of the average on upgrades and improvements. Yet, even with your astounding luck, squinty-eyed frugality and the implication that your house still has pink Formica counter tops, we're going to assume it has appreciated! Yes!

Let's assume all the fairy tales are true (and ignore the real facts).

Where does that leave you, the potential house buyer in the best of all possible situations?

Keep working harder, Jurgis, and the house will make a profit!

Final Profit	
Value of house	$ 269,570
Tax benefits	$ 24,000
Deferred Rent	$ 468,000
Costs (from above)	$1,078,338
TOTAL	$ -316,768

Oh dear. Our example house lost over $300,000 despite our unrealistically meager accounting. Meanwhile you, the house buyer, spent 30 years dealing with debilitating payments, crazy neighbors, forgone vacations, sunken concrete, vintage appliances, and missed opportunities for lucrative investment and savings, not to mention all the things you might have done with that time and money.

30 years of listening to your spouse or partner(s) grumble about the lack of space for a workshop in the sagging garage, or the tiny closets, or lack of a first-floor bathtub.

30 years of getting up at 3am to check on the garage door or sump pump. Learning a million tedious and mundane "skills" that added little or nothing to your enjoyment of life: how to replace faucet washers and cartridges, how to mix gas and oil for the leaf blower, the safest place to put the ladder to clean the gutters, where to find the cheapest and most reliable plumber or the lumber yard with the best deals on treated lumber and hinges. 30 years of leaving work early a couple times a month to pick up mole traps or ice melt or paint or caulk.

Numberless Saturdays patching the driveway, fixing screens, replacing toilet kits, trimming trees, listening to the neighbor kid rattle the windows with the stereo in his 20-year-old car.

All that time. All that effort. All that money. All the things you missed out on.

All of this with the vague idea in the back of your head that you were "saving" somehow, investing, that every hour spent tapping the garage door opener with a hammer and fighting that old screen door was an investment in your future.

Thirty years. And you *lost* $316,768. *At least* $316.768. (Recall that we rounded down most costs and didn't even include a few hundred thousand dollars' worth of likely costs in our total.)

Who knows what you might have accomplished with all the extra time and money if you hadn't been driving from hardware store to hardware store looking for a matching knob for the kitchen cabinet?

Maybe you could have invested all that money you foolishly sunk into concrete vanity tops and extra insulation. Your cousin in Texas who always rented a apartment spent years trying to convince you to invest in oil exploration corporations. You never had the extra money.

He did. He invested rather than buying a house. He has an island now. His own island.

Think about this question for a minute:

If buying and owning houses is such a great investment then why don't the banks just buy all the houses and rent them to us rather than loaning us money to buy them ourselves?

Possible answers:

-Maybe, financing, owning and mainlining a house costs much more than any potential profit?

-Maybe effort-free interest and generous transaction fees are much more lucrative than house owning?

-Maybe the house pushers use your money and your hard work to create value and make money for themselves?

-Maybe the real estate, finance, development and improvement industries put so much time and effort into spreading the Myth of the Happy Homeowner because almost no one would finance houses if they knew the real facts?

Think about it.

Chapter 3 take-aways:
- Houses can't be counted on to appreciate in the same useful way that real investments do.
- Ignore the myths and hype and lay advice. Actual verifiable facts are your friend when evaluating house costs.
- The Mortgage Interest Deduction doesn't "make money." At best it just slows your losses a bit.
- The Property Tax Deduction doesn't "make money." At best it just slows your losses a bit.
- Landlords don't always make money, and even when they do that doesn't prove financing a house is cheaper than renting the same house for the average consumer.
- You may "have to live somewhere" but financing a house will cost much more than most people think and in the vast majority of situations it will cost more than renting.
- Unless you stay in the same house for more than 30 years, don't upgrade or remodel, with no second mortgage, your house costs are no more "locked in" than rent.
- People who try to feed you myths contrary to the above facts and try to convince you that houses are investments that will make you long term profit are lying to you whether they know it or not.

A Real World Example

The house pushing industries are very large, very rich, and recruit new blood and further riches through BS and obfuscation. So let's not just give them our best and fairest numbers, even skewed to their benefit, and walk away.

The fair and balanced numbers we've provided in our ongoing string of house calculations are for you, the faithful reader of this book. We know you're keen of mind, pure of heart, and intend to make decisions about where to call home with an eye toward frugality and common sense.

However, if the house pushers want a target, let's set it up way over there. That way we can sit back safely and watch the fireworks.

So let's go beyond our fair and balanced, conservative, optimistic, middle-ground numbers. Let's work up some real-world, dysfunctional, drama-filled, average American consumer, people-next-door kind of numbers and see what house buying looks like to most people in the house market.

Dear House-Pushing Lobby: Please attack and sue this target. Thanks!

For this example our hypothetical house buyers are an average American family, told by their bank that their household income of $52,000 is sufficient to purchase a $200,000 house.

These folks can only afford to put $10,000 down (borrowed from family) so they will have to purchase PMI at a high rate. That $10,000 will have to be paid back, by the way.

Similarly, their 680 credit rating and low down payment earn them a (currently lousy) 5% interest rate.

Like most Americans they pay too much income tax and see their yearly return of overpaid taxes as a "bonus." Thinking they're being responsible, this family will sink their tax return of about $3,000 into the house every year.

Since they can't afford private schools but want better for their kids, they're buying in a good school system and know their property tax rate will be higher than most.

Their occasional financial windfall gets channeled into "upgrades" that (they believe) will increase the value of their house. They use a modest insurance settlement, for example, to

A Real World Example

build a sunroom and a basement rec room.

They don't have a pension and only one small 401k, but over time they will also install an above-ground pool, outdoor patio with a built in grill, granite counter tops, tile floors, and a basement bathroom when their teens move their bedrooms downstairs. The basement work is paid for by a "home improvement loan" (a second mortgage) they take out during their ninth year of house ownership.

This second mortgage loan is for $22,000 at 5.5%, canceling out much of the small amount of equity they had built up.

They will replace all the appliances twice, except the dishwasher and garbage disposal which are replaced three times. They "upgrade" their roof and windows at year 12 after family members (and a slick salesperson) convince them that a local remodeling company's work will save energy and "increase the value of their home."

> My favorite neighbor: *"They won the lottery, twice, and it's the only way they bought a house in this area. The grandfather is a karaoke enthusiast and has built himself a "sound proofed" karaoke shed in the back garden, right behind my house. It is not sound proofed. The strains of (badly sung) Johnny Cash and Elvis ruin every summer evening because for some reason he only practices when the weather is good. Also the father is a serious alcoholic. Stumbles out to his car, blind stinking drunk at two in the afternoon. Drunk drive to the grocery store for more booze. Drive home, honk at crossing guards blocking the intersection while kids walk home from school. Get drunk and decide to water his lawn. Spray water at and verbally harass anyone walking buy. Yes, I've called the cops to report him when he was harassing others or driving drunk, but they always arrived after he was out of the car or back in the house."*

Sadly, their neighborhood is slowly declining. While the area is still a safe, decent place to live, the big local employer has outsourced many jobs and the local university can't compete with Big Ten University in Capital City. People with money are moving away. Their formally nice school system is cutting back.

At year 14, just as their oldest child starts as a freshman at the community college, a crisis hits. The largest local company has sold out to a big conglomerate and is closing its local facility, so the family's primary bread winner will be out of work. The family faces the loss of two-thirds of their income. The other spouse has a fungible service job so the family discusses relocating where the primary bread winner has better job opportunities.

The family contacts a Realtor® about selling the house. Bad news. They discover their house is underwater. Even though they have paid $19,668 in PMI, $43,200 in property taxes, $14,400 in insurance, $195,840 in principle and interest, and approximately $57,200 in repairs and upgrades to the house over 14 years, our family is shocked to realize they still owe $144,905 on the primary and secondary mortgages. Even more shocking, the Realtor® estimates the house is only worth about $155,000 in the newly depressed local market as many dozens of houses are coming on the market. Closing costs to sell will run about 8% ($12,400) of that $155,000.

This means their "$200,000 house" has cost the family $330,280 so far, and has become a $155,000 house with a $157,305 liability.

The Realtor® agrees to optimistically list the property at $160,000, and to limit his commission if it sells for less, so that the family can "break even." Business is good for the real estate brokers in this newly bleak economy as so many houses change hands.

The family decides they can't afford to sit and wait for the old house to sell. A job opportunity in another city will mean a 10% increase in family income as opposed to the 65% loss they currently face. Waiting could mean the loss of this opportunity. After all the recent calamities, they feel it's critical to lock in this income. They decide to cash in their small 401k (at a significant loss) and use the proceeds to fund their living expenses, allow the primary breadwinner to relocate, and to help them buy a new family home in their new city while the old home is still up for sale.

Two months later the primary bread winner has taken the new job and is staying with a family member in the new city, but the rest of the family is still in the old house. They have received no reasonable offers on their old house. The family makes a weekend trip to the new city where they reunite and another Realtor® shows them houses similar to their old house. The family is again shocked, this time because smaller, more modest houses in the booming new city cost significantly more than what their old house is worth.

Two weeks later the family goes house hunting in the new city again. This time they find a house they really like. It's in a great school district though it lacks the pool and upgraded kitchen. However, it has a nice walkout basement and adjoins a park. The family has been living apart for three months now and is very anxious to settle into their new life together. With their newly increased income and the funds from the 401k, they decide they can afford to buy this $245,000 house.

The family uses $30,000 from their 401k[50] as a down payment, keeping back other funds for closing costs,

---

50 The family will lose approximately 27% of their 401k up front in penalties and taxes, plus they will lose all the potential earnings.

A Real World Example

If houses make so much money then we'll really clean up by paying for two houses!

moving expenses and updates they want to make to the new house. They keep the last $10,000 from the 401k in reserve out of concern for the situation with the old house. The $30,000 down payment on the new house is still less than 20% so they have to pay PMI. Again. Their existing old house mortgages give them a high debt to income ratio so they end up with a less-than-optimum mortgage interest rate of 5.2%. Their Realtor® tells them not to worry; they can refinance later when the old house is sold and things have settled into place.[51]

Two months later the family has moved into their new house in the new city. To their relief, the other spouse has also managed to find a great new job, with full benefits, at a 15% salary increase. The kids like their new school. Things are looking up!

Except… their old house hasn't sold. The loss of the big facility in their old neighborhood has proven to be an even worse economic blow than anyone predicted. Other businesses near their old house have closed in a domino effect and many former neighbors are just walking away from their houses, further devastating the housing market. The eldest son who stayed behind to continue attending college has now moved into the old house to save money.

The Realtor's® contract on the old house is about to end and he makes it clear he doesn't want to renew under the same terms. He feels the house is worth no more than $145,000 in the new market and after six months of fruitless work, he is no longer comfortable with his "lower commission" agreement. He is willing to renew, but only if the family agrees to the new lower price and his full commission.

The family is settling into their new life and their new

---

51 Of course that never happens.

A Real World Example

house. They are updating the kitchen and adding a bathroom in the walkout. Increasingly, the old house seems like a burden and an unwelcome reminder of things that are past. Making payments on both houses is draining their savings faster than they can replace the money.

> My favorite neighbor: *"He is a hoarder and at night when the lights are on inside the house you can see the stacks of stuff piled to the ceiling so that almost no light escapes the window. He must have made a mess of the kitchen because he keeps his groceries in the trunk of his Hyundai and eats out of it. In the summer he'll sit on his front steps with his trunk open and eat sandwiches with the birds eating extra bread next to him."*

The eldest child has moved a couple of roommates into the old house. This college-age child wants to help pay the bills and give a leg up to a couple college buddies at the same time. Between the savings from the student's rent, and the income from two friends, the old house is now only losing $300 each month. (At least for now, until it needs repairs.) If the family sells the old house for $145,000, however, they will lose all the money they have invested, plus the $10,000 they still owe, plus the Realtor's® fees. As long as their student can live in the house, they decide to just eat the $300 per month in extra costs and keep the house as a rental for their student and his friends.

Nine months after the job loss, the family's finances are starting to feel normal again. The new, larger house payments don't seem like such a burden. The $300 per month they have to pay toward the old house seems like a better alternative than writing a check for at least $22,000 to sell the house at a huge loss. In the spring, the eldest child transfers credits to State University. That child will need to live on campus now, to qualify for financial aid with an on-campus job. The roommates want to stay at the old house, and to recruit a third friend to replace the child.

The new status quo has become comfortable. The family has managed to defer the most drastic consequences of their housing debacle by ignoring it. Renting to the students and throwing away $300 a month has allowed them to mostly ignore their underwater house.

Their housing crisis has presented itself in small stages, each stage fairly easy to handle, each leading inevitably a bit further downhill. (Uh oh. When you read that sort of foreshadowing you just *know* something bad is going to happen.)

The family decides to let the students stay. But only for one more year, because obviously this can't go on forever. Maybe in a year housing prices will go back up? When the eldest child moves out, a third roommate moves in. The eldest child promises to check in on the house and friends every so often. A friendly former neighbor agrees to keep an eye on things as well.

A Real World Example

One Sunday morning a couple of months later the family receives a call from the police in their old city. Their old house was the scene of a large party the previous night. Numerous students were cited for under-age drinking. There were some minor drug charges. The authorities can't find any record that the house is licensed as a student rental. Can the family provide information regarding their rental licensing, inspections, and the lease agreements with the students who hosted this illegal party? They are especially concerned with the newest renter. It turns out this "student" isn't even in college, isn't yet 18 years old, and can't legally sign contracts at all. Plus, state law specifically prohibits renting property to students under 21 old without a parent co-signing the lease. The police would like to talk to the family about all of this, and the various citations, as well as the property damage to an adjoining neighbor's house. Civil suits follow.

By the time our example family is finished cleaning up this mess, they have learned more about landlord/tenant law and liability than they ever wanted to know. The various citations and the damage to the (no longer friendly) neighbor's property costs over $3,000. Another $7,500 goes to an attorney in their old city to defend the family against a suit by the parents of the students arrested for under-age drinking, and the forfeiture proceedings that result from the drug charges. The family's insurance carrier threatens to cancel their house policy since their coverage was for a homestead, not a rental. The company denies the claims for damage to the old house, and the change in coverage almost doubles the premiums. The uninsured damage to the old house costs the family another $4,000. Clearly it's time for the old house to go no matter what the cost.

Their original Realtor® is the easiest contact for the distant family and agrees to list the house again, this time for $140,000, as soon as the various repairs and legal proceedings are completed. Meanwhile, the house sits empty again, generating no income to offset the mortgage and other payments. It has been 14 months since the job loss that led to the family's move.

The family accepts a full price offer for the house the first week it's on the market, now feeling irritated that the Realtor® wouldn't list the house for a higher price, and sooner. The closing costs for this underwater sale use up the rest of their emergency fund money and a bit more.

Possibly the worst moment of the entire process was writing that large check at closing; paying someone to take their house, rather than receiving payment for the house. But after 16 months, they're finally free of the old house and able to focus on their new lives in the new city.

```
First house costs
    Mortgage payments              ($ 195,840)
    2nd Mortgage                   ($  28,754)
    Still owe on house             ($ 144,905)
    Borrowed money                 ($  10,000)
    PMI                            ($  19,668)
    Taxes                          ($  56,200)
    Property Insurance             ($  18,200)
    Repairs                        ($  42,500)
    Upgrades                       ($  46,000)
    Rental debacle                 ($  16,000)
    401K loss                      ($  31,000)
    Closing costs [buy & sell]     ($  15,900)
    Cost of $200,000 house:        ($ 549,567)
    First house investment loss    ($ 129,732)
    First house cost               ($ 692,299)

First house profit
    Value of house                 $ 140,000
    Tax benefits                   $   1,200
    Student rent                   $   7,800
    Deferred rent                  $ 242,000
Subtotal Profit                    $ 383,000
Subtotal Cost                      ($692,299)
Out of pocket total loss           ($ 309,099)
```

The family keeps their second house for 19 years. They feel they learned valuable lessons from their first house and vow not to overspend on their second. However, as their remaining children leave the house the couple finishes updating the kitchen and adds a solarium over the patio area. They tile both bathrooms and the entry hall, and convert one of the now-empty bedrooms into an office/hobby room with a sliding door leading to deck overlooking the park. In addition to cooking together in their new gourmet kitchen, the couple spends increasing amounts of time (and money) on elaborate landscaping and gardening.

During year four of their mortgage their youngest child suffers a major health crisis that leads to academic and financial problems. The couple takes out a home equity loan for $15,000 to enable the child to

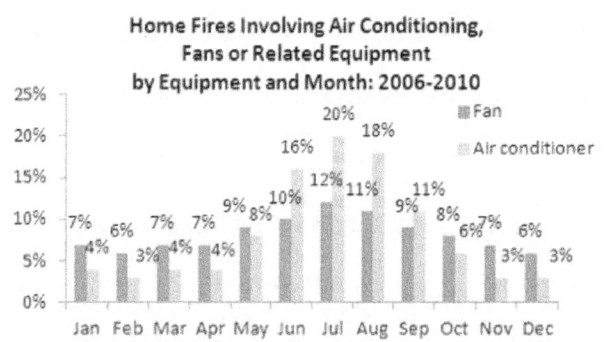

FYI: A very large percentage of such fires are due to poor maintenance or shoddy DIY repairs.

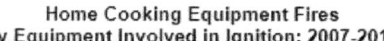
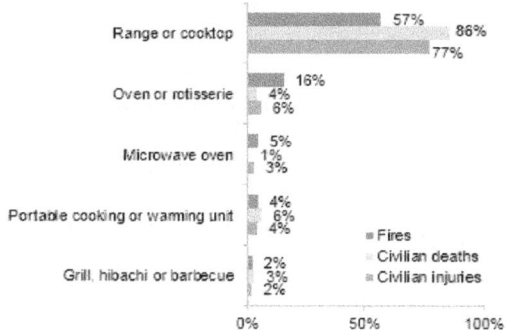

avoid bankruptcy and complete work on a degree at State College.

During year 11 their basement floods while they're on vacation visiting one of their grown children who is getting married. The sump pump fails and the basement fills with water, ruining their washer and dryer, the furnace, the water heater, the furniture in the family room and bedrooms, the carpet, and several boxes of personal belongings. The water shorts out the electric breaker box, turning off power to the entire house. All of the food in their refrigerator and freezer is ruined. The electrical short destroys their laptop computer, the circuit board in the dishwasher, and their new flex-screen television. The sprinkler system runs from an electric timer so when the power goes off some of their expensive landscaping dies.

Though the couple purchased flood insurance specifically out of concern for their lower-level living area, they're shocked to discover that their policy doesn't cover any of the flood damage. They failed to purchase a "sump pump rider" which would have covered the specific sort of problem they experienced and the damage they sustained. The couple decides to minimize costs by leaving the basement area uncarpeted and mostly unfurnished (as just a basement) since they rarely use the space now that their children are gone. Even with that concession, the total bill for the water damage is $17,500.

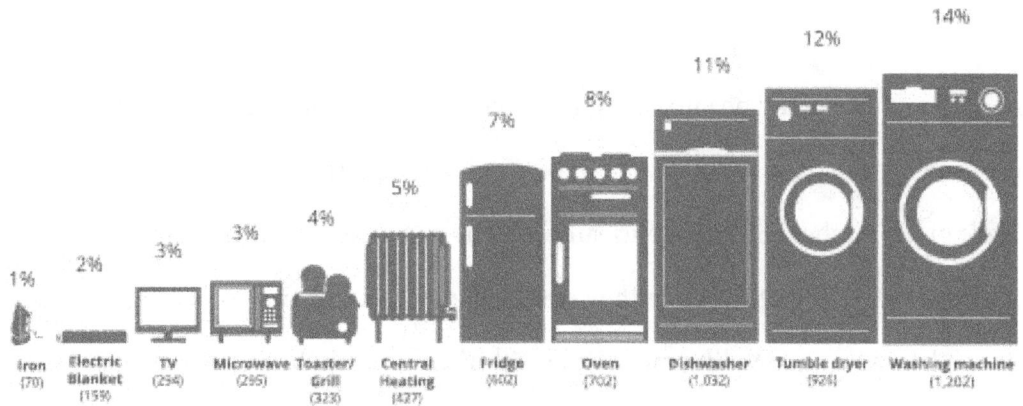

Which appliance is most likely to set *your* house on fire?

(http://www.ifsecglobal.com/what-appliance-is-most-likely-to-set-fire-to-your-home/)

A Real World Example

When the primary bread winner turns 65, the couple sells the house and moves to the Sunbelt. They both face health problems and are tired of the harsh climate. They intend to relocate to an inexpensive rural area in a southern state near one of their grown children, seeing this as the best use of their fixed income.

Thanks to their new city's flourishing economy the second house has treated them much better than the first, appreciating on average at 1% per year above inflation despite 1) a devastating 25% loss precipitated by a housing "crash" during year eleven of the mortgage, and 2) their value-diminishing decision to leave the lower level "unfinished" and so with fewer bedrooms than when they purchased the house. Though they suffered a large loss overall, they leave the closing with a check and (like most house owners) with the misconception that their house had "made money."

```
Second house costs
    Mortgage:                        ($   269,040)
    2nd Mortgage                     ($    21,811)
    Still owe on house               ($   116,477)
    PMI                              ($    11,825)
    Taxes                            ($    77,900)
    Property Insurance               ($    26,600)
    Repairs                          ($    57,500)
    Upgrades                         ($    52,000)
    Closing costs                    ($    28,820)
    Opportunity cost from house #2   ($   376,473)
    Cost of $245,000 house:          ($ 1,384,446)

Second house profit
    Value of house                   $    299,000
    Tax benefits                     $      7,350
    Deferred rent                    $    364,000
Subtotal Profit                      $    681,150
Subtotal Cost                        ($ 1,384,446)
Out of pocket lost:                  ($   367,296)

Running total investment loss        ($   506,205)[52]
```

Just imagine. This couple could be entering into retirement with a bit over a half million extra dollars from investing even at the modest estimate of a 5% ROI on a long term investment strategy over 33 years. Instead, they have given up that $506,205, plus suffered out-of-pocket losses from both houses, putting their total loss over 33 years at $1,126,387. All so they could spend their free time on crabgrass and caulk rather than, say, starting a business or spending more time with their kids or chasing some dream.

---

[52] (If the family had been investing since they bought the first house and continued to invest through the ownership of the second house this is the total, cumulative investment they would now have.)

A Real World Example

House #3, their southern retirement house, will be their last.

They pay $160,000 for a modest but immaculate "move-in ready" house in a Home Owners Association neighborhood with access to a small lake, golf course, pool and a community center. Their large $45,000 down payment and improved credit scores earn them a great interest rate and negate the need for PMI.

Their HOA fees are a bit high, $1500 per year, because of the neighborhood's extra amenities. Taxes and insurance (combined in an escrow account) in this locale are lower than the national average, however, only another $1800 annually. The couple spends $17,400 right after move-in upgrading the kitchen, outdoor grill area, and master suite. During the 14 years they live in their retirement house they spend only a couple thousand dollars a year on convenience and safety upgrades, landscaping, and (after one of them suffers a fall) some accessibility alterations.

In year 14 the former primary breadwinner dies. The remaining spouse isn't healthy and decides the best course is to sell the house and relocate to a senior apartment with 24/7 on site management.

The house appraises for $210,000 (about 1.25% appreciation overall).

Retirement house costs	
Mortgage:	$ 128,184
Still owe on house	$ 83,589
Taxes	$ 28,000
Property Insurance	$ 21,500
HOA fees	$ 21,000
Repairs	$ 49,500
Upgrades	$ 26,500
Closing costs	$ 16,540
Opportunity cost	$ 154,044
Cost of $160,000 house:	$ 418,857
Retirement house profit	
Value of house	$ 210,000
Tax benefits	$ 5,030
Deferred rent	$ 168,000
Subtotal Profit	$ 383,030
Subtotal Cost overall	$ 418,857
Out of pocket loss	(-$ 38,827)
Investment plus house loss	($1,163,341)[53]

Of course, at the remaining spouse's last house sale our remaining hypothetical family won't see this complete and accurate accounting. Who would provide that for them?

---

[53] The cumulative total of the investment loss plus the 3rd house loss

Because they're not financially sophisticated, and because they didn't look beyond the house-pusher's rhetoric, this family never realized they lost out on at least $506,205 over the course of 33 years before they retired. Plus the $676,395 in out of pocket losses for the first two house. Plus the out of pocket loss of $32,827 on the third house.

Remember that's still without counting hundreds of thousands of dollars in additional expenses and 401k losses that could have been invested, and only counting on a 5% ROI for potential long term investments, and completely cashing them out of their investment when they retired instead of living from the interest on the investment.

If their goal was to create an inheritance for their kids they could have kept the investment rolling during their retirement and, still using a modest 5% ROI, their total investment lost would be $1,127,514 plus the $700,000 out-of-pocket loss on the three houses. That's close enough to two million dollars to cause most people to gasp.

If the nice folks at the <u>Wall Street Journal</u> and <u>Forbes</u> are correct that long term investments could generate a 8% ROI, this family would have earned $3,074,095 over 48 years if they had invested wisely rather than just following the path of house financing. They gave all that money and opportunity to someone else.

Worse they traded that money for the trials and tribulations of babysitting a big pile of deteriorating wood instead of using their money to improve their lives and the lives of their children.

Chapter 4: No More "Man of the Castle"

Pride of Ownership

So you're not likely to become the next Mark Zuckerberg by sitting at home and paying your mortgage on time. Losing money seems inevitable. Houses are an expense, not an investment. Got it.

So what are good non-financial reasons to buy a house? Now that we've seen that house-ownership is a cash-your-paycheck-at-the-casino- level financial disaster, why would anyone want to buy one?

"Pride of ownership is the number one reason why people yearn to own their home."

Is that true?

What does it mean?

Well, the quote comes from a "home buying" website (There's that infuriating insistence upon conflating "houses" and "homes" again), courtesy of a writer described as a "Home Buying/Selling Expert" (Pretentiously Capitalized Title, theirs).

But let's not pick on the "Home Buying/Selling Expert" or "home buying BS.com;" this is a very common house-buying justification. You'll see that claim scattered throughout house-pushing literature. This claim is as ubiquitous as sodium or high-fructose corn syrup in fast food.

While it's hard to determine the truth value of such a purposely vague claim, we can be forgiven for asking (as we just did): what the hell does "pride of ownership" even mean?

Isn't it possible, for example, to be proud of *not* owning a house? In the same way you might be proud to have dodged a bullet by not marrying that brittle, needy hottie from high school who ended up cooking meth and then getting tasered by the cops live on FOX News?

We'll call it "pride of not-making-bad-choices."

Psychologists tell us that people can be persuaded to derive pride from almost anything, given enough positive reinforcement. So house buying might indeed provide

> *"I am patient with stupidity but not with those who are proud of it."*
> --Edith Sitwell

perverse pride to some people, like jail house tattoos or DUIs or avoidable scars do for other people. This pride doesn't make any of those things smart ideas.

Also, what's with this pompous sounding concept of "ownership?" Right now I'm feeling some pride of authorship. Are you feeling pride of readership? You might even be glowing with pride of downloadership for having made this smart buyership decision. Highfivership!

Let's be blunt. The phrase "pride of ownership" just reeks of overblown, focus-group marketing. "Proud to own?" No. Doesn't sound profound enough. Hmmm. Hey, what about "pride of ownership?" Test that one!

Owning a house will make all my dreams come true! As long as I dream about debt, work and stress.

Oh wait. Here is what our self-appointed Home Buying/Selling Expert means by "Pride of Ownership:"

"It means you can paint the walls any color you desire, turn up the volume on your CD player, attach permanent fixtures and decorate your home according to your own taste. Home ownership gives you and your family a sense of stability and security. It's making an investment in your future."

"Paint the walls any color you desire?" Well now we're excited. All for the small price of between $500,000 and a million large, and the best years of your life. That better be one hell of an amazing shade of "Autumn Butterscotch."

Except, of course, that this freedom really applies universally only to the interior walls. Your HOA or local Historic District might have something to say about painting the exterior walls. Depending upon where you live, one of these friendly entities might dictate your color choice, whether you can paint yourself or must hire someone, and whether that someone must be the association president's brother-in-law.

It's also worth noting that, even as a house owner, if you want to channel that weird phase you went through at 15 and paint your interior walls black and purple, you'll likely have to spend more money repainting them later. Gail® will twist your arm until you paint everything neutral colors when you go to sell. She'll make fun of you at the

> My favorite neighbor: *"The elderly man who seems to live alone solely with his dog. Every day you can catch them out for a walk. The problem was that his dog will poo in the street and instead of picking it up, he uses one of those extended tennis ball throwers to flick the poo INTO PEOPLE'S YARDS. We dubbed him as 'Poo Flicker'."*

Congressional fundraiser, too.

Besides, many renters have allowance to paint. Our Home Expert leads their pro-house discussion with this weak paint argument?

We could ridicule the "CD player" comment too, but that's low-hanging fruit. The really noteworthy aspect of this music-related crap is the laughable idea that you can't turn up music as a renter, and can do so as a house owner. I'm glad that the Home Buying/Selling Expert isn't my landlord. Or my neighbor.

In our humble experience, any residence that can regulate someone's music—dorm room, apartment, house in a neighborhood, condo, mobile home, army barracks, RV park—has specific rules regarding "quiet times."

So, sorry, no blasting your old Run DMC CDs at 2am, even if you own a house. The neighbors will toss dog poo on your car and call the cops on a noise violation.

We're not sure what all the excitement is about regarding "attaching permanent fixtures," either. Did our Expert spend some time in prison? People unused to incarceration don't usually get that wound-up contemplating hanging towel bars and shelves.

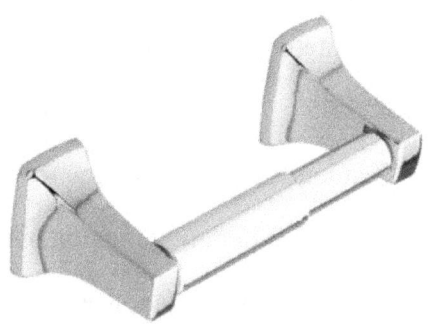

I am fulfilled. I am complete.

Next our Expert declares: "home ownership gives you and your family a sense of stability and security."

We have to admit, that description can be pretty accurate, as far as it goes. Unfounded beliefs, even false and foolish ones, certainly can give a sense of security and stability to those who believe.

In the same way that the belief in faith healing allows people to feel better, even as they're dying by degrees, and a belief in "winning streaks" gives gamblers a sense of security as they double down on black with borrowed money, belief in the Myth of The Happy Homeowner seems to make certain people feel comfortable even as they piss away hundreds of thousands of dollars and decades of their lives.

Sad. But true.

But this seems more like an observation about human nature and psychology than about houses. "Behold! People are gullible!"

I believe!

Do we need to say anything more about the "investment in your future" nonsense? Except maybe to note, again, the careful wording. Our Expert doesn't really make any specific claims. This vague remark just leaves an odor of fiscal opportunity that lingers in the air.

How do we reconcile "investment in your future" with losing hundreds of thousands of dollars? It sounds to us like a deliberate attempt to mislead. Commonly known as a "lie."

It is all sort of like a casino, actually. Myths. Implied promises. Desperate hope. An unfounded sense of optimism. And the lingering smell of false opportunity.

At least at the casino sometimes the drinks are free.

Neighbors: Fellow Travelers in Hell

As noted, buying a house binds you, the house buyer, to the land.

That land continues, by the way, beyond the dying hydrangea and fields of dandelions and connects you with a motley assortment of other people who made equally stupid mistakes and bought the houses that surround you. These unpleasant strangers are your neighbors.

If you buy a house these neighbors now share your fate. You share theirs. Think of them like "friends" on an eerie 3D Facebook account you cannot shut down, peopled seemingly by those chosen for their offensive and annoying quirks.

Except that these disturbing strangers are real and they're here and they're so close you'll hear their domestic violence.

They, in turn, will be peering through your windows, listening to your arguments, picking up your garbage from their driveways and witnessing your every mistake and embarrassment for decades. At best.

At worst, they'll be digging through your garbage, stealing your garden gnomes, and posting online videos of your little sister taken through the bathroom window when she visits.

You, for your part, will spend years listening to your neighbors flush their toilets and start their aging cars outside your bedroom window each weekday morning. Each and every morning. Like malevolent clockwork.

Who knows what other surprises await? Neighbors collect rows of old bicycles. Neighbors unlawfully keep pigs in their garage. Neighbors arise at 4am to power-blow leaves out of their gutters. Neighbors do very, very odd things. You may have inadvertently adopted-by-proximity an elderly or obese neighbor with a fondness for fresh air and a laissez faire attitude about clothing and personal hygiene. Or maybe you live next to a family who rescues dozens of large vicious dogs or has a troubled child that wakes up screaming each night.

Its licensed and insured and every chicken has a driver's license so you can't make me get rid of it!

After all, every manner of dysfunctional person you've ever seen on live newscasts being tackled by the cops has to live somewhere. Interesting folks like professional yodelers, people with a fondness for huge, homemade, lighted wind chimes, paranoid gun-toting last-days survivalists digging shelters under the gazebo, people trying to power their houses using fermented chicken droppings, crazy cat ladies, even crazier ferret and llama ladies, that kid you read about who tried to make a nuclear reactor in his parent's shed and ended up irradiating the entire neighborhood... the world is full of people who deal with life on completely different terms than you and the place they do it to its fullest bug-nutty extent is in their houses and yards.

Right next to your house and your yard.

Chained like a Dog to a Tree

For some odd reason many people assume buying a house will free them from neighbor problems. *"Let's buy a house and move away from those awful people living upstairs!"*

Notice the internal contradiction and unexamined assumptions that underlie this faulty reasoning? In other words; that's crazy talk!

First, observe the wonderful freedom to be able to move away and escape a crazy and unpleasant neighbor. The speaker of that italicized sentence seems to be saying: "It's good to have the option of escaping a horrible person! So let's remove that option and chain ourselves to a place we can't escape!

Buying a house--at best—makes the option of fleeing an unpleasant, dangerous, or unmanageable situation a couple orders of magnitude more difficult. At worst, escape becomes all—but impossible.

That's the reason neighbors merit an entire section. Buying a house shackles you to neighbors. Both you, and they, are stuck together to a degree difficult to imagine if you've never owned a house next to someone who defies all description.

"But," the inexperienced might foolishly protest: "I can still move! If the situation gets too out of hand I'll just sell my house and get another."

Technically true. But this is very much like getting married to someone you've met only on the Internet under the logic that "you can always get divorced if things don't work out."

Selling a house, like entering a marriage, is a huge and very expensive project.

Remember all the money you'll tie up in buying your house?

Now, when you want to sell it, a real estate broker will take another 6% or 7% of your selling price right off the top. In our $200,000 example that's $12,000 to $14,000. Not including moving expenses or surveys, home inspections, and repairs necessary for selling the house.

Plus you're sacrificing any money you've already tied up in the place. As we discussed earlier in the book, a typical home mortgage arrangement has you spending well over 90% of your money on taxes, insurance and interest for many years. In other words, you can live in a house, spend tens of thousands of dollars on it, and, if you need to sell after only a few years, be shocked to discover you owe almost as much on the house as when you started.

In fact, it's usually much cheaper and easier to divorce that charming online stranger who turned out to be a raging, violent serial killer than it is to sell the house you bought next door to them.

Imagine a situation so bad you'd consider taking a $40,000 or $60,000 loss in order to escape a person who lived beside you.

What would it take? An acrimonious, years-long series of lawsuits? Bodies buried in the backyard? A dozen large pit bull/hyena mixes

chained to your fence? Your tires slashed, your windows broken, your ferret poisoned, your kids followed to school, your mail stolen, your garden ornaments vandalized, and threatening calls made to your boss?

With such obviously hostile behavior going on next door, who is going to buy your house?

House-buying propaganda has created a myth of the All-American Main Street. Tree-lined avenues, lovely lawns, well-kept houses, a nice new car in each driveway. Each home peopled with a friendly, retired couple planning their next vacation, or a prosperous young family hosting dinner parties for their equally respectable friends. Maybe a knock on your door as you move in, an offer of help or a tray of brownies. Solid members of the community pulling together for the benefit of all.

Actually, we're Jewish but Ma bought us these outfits just for your barn-raising!

Your daughter looking for a summer job? The folks across the street might be able to get her a spot in the Governor's office. Raising a barn? The neighbors will pitch in and show up wearing Amish garb, hammers and saws in hand.

In this fantasy world, people unlike you don't own houses. Nope. If you love BBQ, all your neighbors will have huge built-in grills with smokers and pizza ovens. They will line up outside your door with their favorite sauces, rubs and sure-fire recipes.

If you're a vegetarian, your neighbors will be, too. No danger of awaking on a clear spring morning to the smell of flesh searing on a fire, the charred smoke drifting through your bedroom window and filling your entire home.

Love music? Your neighbors will too! And by some amazing coincidence they'll all love the same sort of alt/folk/rap you enjoy, played at top volume. Unless you like it quiet. Then they will be mute.

Are you a late sleeper? There's absolutely no chance the people next door like to get up on weekends at 6am and fire up varieties of power equipment you never knew existed.

People who own houses don't have loud, unmuffled motorcycles. Do they? Or huge, jacked up 4x4 trucks that spew mud and fumes all over your roses when they park drunk in

Why look, Darling. Our new neighbors must enjoy cycling.

your lawn at 3am.

People who own houses really don't spend hundreds of dollars growing heirloom rosebushes that are super sensitive to dog piss and diesel exhaust fumes. Right…?

Doesn't everyone love NASCAR? And cello music? Won't my neighbors be so grateful when I set up the projector and speakers in the back yard for my Super Bowl party? They can watch right out their windows!

What could go wrong?

> **My favorite neighbor:** *"My neighbor Jim is a really nice old senile man, and is convinced that pissing on clothing and hanging it on posts in his garden keeps the deer away. I don't really know if it works or not but its peculiar seeing a bunch of piss soaked clothing hanging from his garden."*

The Man

"A man's home is his castle."

That cliché sounds amazingly dated these days, and not just because women now own their own houses.

The real issue with this tired old truism is that it isn't true, because if you finance a house "your" new house really isn't entirely "yours." Your mortgage company has a lot to say about how you might use your house. And since you mortgaged it you also had to purchase mandatory insurance. Your insurance carrier has even more to say about what you do and don't do with your house.

We'd guess your house is located in a nation, in a state, in a county, and in some municipality or hamlet. So that means all these other tax-fed entities have a vested interest in your house as well. And since you likely opted for a place with utility service there are even more quasi-public entities that have rights in your little fiefdom.

Is your house serviced by a public road? Mmmm. Well, that means the local road commission also has some power over your life.

From air space to zoning all sorts of government entities, from the federal down to the township or city level, have the right to mandate or prohibit all sorts of house related things. If you have a Home Owners Association… oh boy. They have as much potential power over the use of your house as you do.[54]

---

54 More about the joys of HOAs later in the book.

So your house really isn't so much "your castle" as it is a sort of a shared public toilet you're occupying for a while.

So be a good citizen. Get your business done quickly, make sure you flush, and don't use the last of the toilet paper. Whatever you do, don't make a mess. Because, though many entities have rights and interests in your house, and power and authority over it, you're the one responsible for cleaning and maintenance.

Mortgage Holders

In addition to charging you $142,456 in interest for your $200,000 house, and requiring you pay for both PMI and a type of homeowners insurance they approve because it's mostly for their benefit, your mortgage holder does even more.

Like a vast, omnipotent, guardian angel, your financial institution is dedicated to watching over your house. And watching over you. If you read the fine print on your mortgage (which no one ever does) you'll find it chock full of restrictions and rules governing all manner of things.

First, you'll discover that the mortgage holder is the earliest and most important guest at the party. If anything goes awry, they stand first in line to get whatever money is available. In front of you, of course. That's why you hear about people who, after paying hundreds of thousands of dollars over many years on a house, still get booted out onto the street without a penny. Where did all their money go? All available money from a house sale goes to the mortgage holder until the mortgage holder decides they have enough money. Surprisingly, they rarely have much left over for you.

Charming note: in most cases, you can't even sell or rent or lease your own house without the mortgage holder's approval. This is because the terms of your

"We can't allow you to rent out your house, no. But we'd be happy to take it back, keep your money and ruin your credit. Of course, we have to charge a fee for that."

mortgage are likely special terms available only to owner-occupied houses. Rentals are often considered a higher risk so the terms may not be as favorable. If you want to rent out your own house you may have to go and ask, hat in hand, if the mortgage holder will be so kind as to charge you more money and give you permission to do what you want with the house you "bought."

As for selling the house while you still owe money: no can do. Most mortgages clearly state that if you even attempt to transfer title to the house while you still owe mortgage holder money you void the mortgage and the entire remaining balance (interest and principle) is due immediately. You write a check for what's left of that $ 342,456 or lose the house. And if you do lose it, guess who gets first dibs on any money the house is worth?

This is the reason that many "rent to own" or "land contract" offers are scams. If the owner of a mortgaged house tries to get you to pay a bit extra each month as part of a "rent to own" scheme, they're likely violating the terms of their own mortgage. Similarly, you can't sell a house with a mortgage on a land contract either.

The only way you can sell your mortgaged house is if the potential buyer has a big fat check cut to pay off your mortgage holder(s) first.

That's really what a "closing" is all about. Such ceremonies are largely just a deal between the old mortgage holder and a new one, with the buyer and seller serving junior roles as stunt doubles and the various third parties collecting check. You're not so much buying a house as you're agreeing to take on the responsibility, debt and financial liability of the previous owner. Plus more. And paying dearly for the privilege.

Again, your mortgage holder has a lot to say about what you

> My favorite neighbor: "We have large trees in our yard. Trees drop leaves. The woman across the street, now known as Leaf Lady to everyone on the street, just can't handle leaves in her yard. We take meticulous care when it's leaf dropping season to keep them cleaned up from the yard and the street, but this isn't enough. Nothing would be I imagine, as we're pretty sure she has OCD. Vacuums her garage daily, washes out her trash bins weekly. For about a year she would come outside, yell and scream while she cleaned up her yard. And then take everything she'd collected, walk across the street, and dump it in our yard. She does the same to the neighbors next door when their tree messes up her yard. We did nothing about it for months, it just amused us. Dumping the offending leaves back in our yards just meant they'd blow back into hers and the futility of it just cracked us up. Then she started waiting in her yard every morning for me to leave for work, and spraying my car down with the hose. Nope. We started telling her to stay off our property. She refused. It escalated to the point I would go out of the garage with our hose in hand and give her three seconds to get her ass off our property. Crazy moved fast enough I never got the chance to actually shoot her in the face with the hose though. She ended up calling the police and saying we were threatening her. Cops came, and before even talking to us wrote her a warning to stay off others property. She'd told them the whole story thinking she was in the right. She still pulls shenanigans but as long as she keeps her crazy on her property no one cares."

do before you sell, while you live in your house. Anything you might do that, in their eyes, could potentially lower the house's value is a big no-no.

They may get a bit concerned when you propose to start ripping things out or tearing things down, even if you've a grand plan to put it all back together later, bigger and better. You take a risk for any funky ideas, especially if you decide to avoid permits and/or zoning, and just push forward with that unauthorized but fantastic DIY project you saw on Pinterest.

Not only do mortgage holders discourage you from cutting up your old roof with a chainsaw and pulling it off with a rope and a pickup truck,[55] they also furrow their sensitive corporate brows when you add fireplaces or wood stoves or pools to your property—any alteration that creates potential liability.[56]

> Online legal resource FindLaw.com conducted a survey about neighbor disputes. The six most common disputes reported:
> - Noise (48% of all disputes). Whether it be from raucous late-night parties or maybe different sleep schedules that result in one neighbor waking up the other, noise is apparently the No. 1 way to annoy your neighbor.
> - Pets and animals (29%). Pets and animals can be tricky to deal with directly, since it is the animal that is causing the problem and not the owner. But many times the issue stems from the owner's failure to properly handle or train his animal.
> - Children's behavior (21%). Much like pets, children running onto your property, being loud, or defacing your property can often be the result of their parents -- i.e., your adult neighbors -- not properly looking after them. State laws may even hold the kids' parents liable for damages.
> - A visual nuisance, the property's appearance, trash, etc. (18%). Many eyesores, such as unkempt lawns, offensive signs, or overflowing trash cans can lead to ill will between neighbors.
> - Property boundaries (17%). In these types of disputes, neighbors often have misconceptions about where their property begins and ends.

The biggest nightmare, however, for a mortgage holder is when you run off and try to create additional debt connected to the house. That puts their 100% guaranteed profits at risk. How can they resell your mortgage and create weird mutant financial instruments based on your debt if you go and do something like that? A second mortgage loan is flat unlawful without the approval of your primary mortgage holder. Even if they do give their permission, this new debt goes behind them in line (but still in front of you).

Similarly, your mortgage holder has made it mandatory for you to pay your taxes on time and keep your house insurance in effect. This is so important that when you

---

55 I did this once. I have pictures. But my house didn't have a conventional mortgage and I had permits.

56 Your insurance carrier is even more interested. More on that soon.

signed all those papers at closing you gave your mortgage holder authority to pay your taxes for you and charge you a handling fee should you let them go unpaid. They can also find and pay for insurance that they choose—even if it costs more—should you let your insurance lapse. And of course they pass this entire cost on to you, plus a fee. Because they're looking out for you.

Insurance Watchdogs

Much like your stalker mortgage overlord, but even more so, your insurance company is very, very interested in you and your house.

It isn't an exaggeration to say that your insurance company cares about everything you do at and with your house. Putting a beer fridge in the basement? Mom moving in? Shopping for a hot tub? Moving the washer and dryer? Planning to plug in your vintage collection of 220v sex toys? Not so fast.

Have you reviewed your homeowners insurance to make certain you can do that?

There are a thousand-and-one things that might unintentionally void your homeowner's policy. You know, the one you're required by your mortgage holder to keep in good standing.

This nosy tag-team is in the business of making money by betting on you and your house. Given how unpredictable humans can be, this business model works much better if they can exert stifling control over you and your house.

"Big Brother" is a rank amateur compared to these private sector interests.

You see, these mortgage and insurance companies are corporations. That means they're free from silly,

annoying limitations like respecting your Constitutional rights and freedoms. All that grade-school-civics-class stuff is only binding on the government. With a few exceptions, corporations are not bound by dull guarantees of your civil liberties. Corporations have the wealth and power of governments with few of the limitations, and all the benefits of being "people," without any of the responsibilities fleshy people have.

You do, of course, have rights and freedoms. You have the right

and freedom—for example—to enter into contracts and so to sign away your other rights and freedoms. Which, if you're a house owner, you already did.

Almost unlimited resources. Permission to track you all the way down to urine tests and DNA samples. No need to respect civil rights or Constitutional protections. And you signed the documents that gave these ~~wankers~~ large and powerful corporations the power to monitor, prohibit, and mandate your behaviors.

You're *paying* them to do that stuff.

According to decades of court records and consumer research, insurance companies can, and do, hire private investigators to follow people, video them, harass their children, interrogate their neighbors, track down former spouses and employers, access medical and DMV records, and otherwise use processes legal and maybe-not-so-legal to acquire pretty much any information they need to satisfy themselves that you're following their rules—or to prove that you're not.

Even their own evidence and testimony proves that insurance companies can, and do, pressure fire departments that have already determined the cause of the house fire, and cleared you of any wrongdoing, to initiate another investigation, and another, and another. And if they still can't find enough support to charge you with arson,[57] they can hire their own fire investigator who will find that support.

Insurance companies can order autopsies of your dead family members. Against your will.

They can confiscate your property and possessions. They can hire the sorts of specialized forensic experts you could only imagine in your wildest dreams to make claims you could not image in your most surreal nightmares.

They can, and do, bring in hired-gun doctors to make medical cases in court.

Insurance companies can, and do, argue both sides of any argument as it suits their purpose, sometimes in the same case, document or paragraph.

Even more entertaining, your insurance company has built into your insurance contract some very useful ambiguity. Your floor wax? Dish detergent? Air freshener? DANGEROUS CHEMICALS! Stored in your house in violation of your policy conditions! No insurance coverage for you!

---

57 So they can avoid paying out on the policy, of course.

Your Pop Tarts®58 toaster pastries? Yep, they're flammable.59 What kind of monster puts flammable material in a toaster in the house where his children live? The insurance company may just have to call Child Protective Services on you if you pursue this claim. Your kid could end up in foster care.

Insurance companies also operate in a strange and rarefied world of special terms they get to define because they make them up.

What? Your basement flooded? Filled with water? Water caused damage? No, your flood insurance won't cover that. "Flood insurance" doesn't cover that kind of water-related-but-not-flood-by-our-definition damage. Didn't you read your policy and hire a corporate law firm to review the dozens of pages of technical legal jargon that doesn't mean what you think it means?

What, did you think we were kidding?

Your beach house was destroyed by a hurricane? No your hurricane damage insurance policy won't cover that. How could we know you'd build that beach house on a beach? Just because you paid for hurricane insurance doesn't mean we knew you'd build in the path of a hurricane. Obviously you're in violation of the "due diligence" and "care and precaution" provisions outlined in your policy. See you in court.60

Don't worry too much, though. Your insurance company isn't likely to come knocking on your door and demanding to look through your underwear drawer . . . unless you file a claim.61

The larger the claim, the more likely your insurance company will rise from its slumbers and turn its searing eyes on you.

---

58 Pop Tarts® is a registered trademark of the Kellogg's©® corporation. Name used here under the Fair Use Doctrine and Geneva Convention. And to warn you the damn things are flammable. All bow to our Pop Tart™ overlords.

59 According to news stories the fire investigator said: "...strawberry Pop-Tarts® when left in a toaster that doesn't pop up, will send flames 'like a blowtorch' up to three feet high." (This book has been such fun to write!) http://articles.latimes.com/1995-02-10/business/fi-30465_1_strawberry-pop-tarts

60 Except, of course, that these days you won't have a chance to go to a court. Modern insurance policies all require "binding arbitration" which means if you disagree with the insurance company you can't go to court, you have to let a non-judicial referee decide the case, a person the insurance company gets to choose. Good luck with that.

61 Some people have noted that paying someone for "protection" in such circumstances has a rather dark history, conjuring up images of guys in loud suits with Tommy Guns. We aren't saying that, we are just informing you that others have said that. We are here to provide you with hilarious information.

Utilities and Roads

Your house is likely sitting on land, and that land is likely bounded by a road on at least one side.

The good news is that while someone paved part of your land, you still own the land under the road! Yep. At least to the middle of the road, in most cases.

The bad news is, while you paid for that land, and pay taxes on it, it does you no good at all. In fact, it has the potential to become a huge nightmare.

Sure, you can walk on it. Drive on it. Ride your bike on it. But so can everyone else. People can stop on it. Stand on it. Stare at you on it, dance provocatively in thongs on it, walk their donkey and allow it to take a 10 lb. dump on it. And there's nothing you can do about any of that. In fact, you're likely responsible for cleaning up the donkey poo.

This is because the local road authority usually has what's referred to as a "right of way" over that land. A right of way is a special sort of "easement."

An easement is a legal right to use property belonging to another. To you, in this case, if you buy a house. Such easements are a really nifty deal for the road authorities because while they get to use your land, you're still responsible for maintaining it and paying taxes on it!

Here is a fairly typical example of the sorts of rights your road authority has over your land because of their right-of-way easement: "the power to cut down trees and other growing things, smooth out curves, expand the traveled portion, and add gravel or pave the roadbed, all without having to ask your permission as long as the work is done within the limits of the easement. The town may also permit others—including power, telephone and cable companies—to use the right-of-way, or may use the easement itself for sewer or water lines."

Typically road authorities can also prohibit you from "building or maintaining structures

> Sec. 6-13 of the ["Hillbilly"] County Code of Ordinances is hereby replaced in its entirety with the following: (a) No dog shall be left unattended outdoors unless it is restrained and restricted to the owner's property by a tether, rope, chain, fence or other device. Fencing, as required herein, shall be adequate in height, construction and placement to keep resident dogs within such fenced area and keep other dogs and children from accessing such fenced area. One (1) or more secured gates to the lot shall be provided."

on the easement, making significant changes to elevations, undertaking substantive alterations that could have the effect of impacting safe public use of the right-of-way…" etc.

In short, this is "your" land. You have a responsibility for keeping it cleaned up and mowed and safe. You pay taxes on it. But the road authority can do whatever they want with it and they can stop you from doing anything they don't like.

They can also give other entities permission to do, and prohibit you from doing, such things.

> "Spite Houses" are houses built to annoy a neighbor or family member, block a view, or challenge a zoning law—an idea that is believed to have originated in the early 1700s. There are also "spite fences." The most troubling part of this idea is that such spite structures are so common they have a special term to describe them and laws to prohibit them.

They've already given nearly every single individual person in the world, all 7,328,735,180 of them, enforceable rights to wander around on this portion of your land with almost no meaningful limitations at all.

You may or may not find it odd that the government, through its step-child the road authority, has all this power over a strip of your land. But you might conceivably find it at least a bit odd that the government's road authority is empowered to re-gift this authority to other quasi-governmental agencies like the water and sewer utilities.

You'll almost certainly find it disturbing that this dictatorial power over your land is then being handed out, willy-nilly, like candy at Halloween, like celebrity sex tapes on the Internet, to private for-profit and public corporations you might not even like or support. Companies like Comcast®, AT&T®, Con Ed®, Google®, or Pacific Power® and their ilk.[62]

Even if you've sworn everlasting vengeance upon Comcast ® (just for example, Comcast ®!) and are determined to boycott until the end of time everything they have ever touched with their cold, evil, leathery fingers, you can't do anything at all to keep them from parking one of their trucks on this part of your land while their evil minions[63] clumsily trim branches from your favorite tree.

Ain't that some shit?

A locally famous California spite house built to block the view of the house behind.

---

62 Ilk is one of those odd words that you only see used for one purpose: to describe people the writer doesn't want you to like.

63 Minions is another of those words.

The infamous "Alameda Spite House." According to popular legend, after the city of Alameda, California claimed a part of Charles Froling's land in the early 20th century and built a road through it, Froling decided to build this 10-foot wide home out of spite.

Similarly, the government, the road authority, the water and sewer utilities, and designated private sector agents (it's just an example, Comcast!®) can all hire contractors who also get to exercise power and authority over your land.

In this way crews of diggers, cutters, pavers, mowers, painters, sweepers, leaf blowers, drillers, wire stringers—strangers of almost every type and description—have been empowered to perform noisy, dangerous, potentially destructive activities on your land pretty much whenever they want to, even if you don't approve.

This amazingly long string of loose and sloppy delegation also means you're never quite sure who might have been tromping around in your roses.

If you come home from vacation and find, for instance, that a large and critical part of your driveway is missing, who do you call? Who is the road authority? County, city, state? Or maybe it was a company one of them hired to tear up the road in preparation for repaving it. Or one of the other subcontractors responsible for rerouting utilities, changing the elevation, or installing hydrants and fixtures. Or the graders and pavers. Or a company tasked with going back and fixing the mess caused by all these other yahoos. In the meantime, how do you get the minivan back in the garage?

Just wait until you try to get a pothole filled.

Ordinances (A Parable)

"Why can't you make them cut it down?" my wife asked the ordinance enforcement officer. "Look at it! It's dead. It's rotten. Pieces of it are falling into my yard."

The officer used his hand to shade his eyes and started up at the huge tree, "Yep. Sure is. And look at the size of it! When that one falls…whoa. That's gonna take out someone's house!"

According to local legend, two brothers inherited land in Boston from their deceased father in 1874. While one brother was away serving in the military, the other brother built a large home on the land, leaving only a tiny plot for his brother. So the solider decided to build this tiny home to block his brother's view and sunlight.

Ordinances (A Parable)

Local legend has it this Seattle spite house, built in 1925, was the result of a couple's divorce: the husband got the house, the wife got the front yard. What better way to spite an ex than with a miniature house as lawn decor? A second version has it that the house was built after a dispute and failed land deal between neighbors.

The tree was over three feet in diameter and rose about 40 feet above the fence like a lone Greek column till it came to an abrupt end where it had apparently sheared off in some past disaster. It was massive and hollow and very, very dead. The tree sat at the corner of the lot, within 25 feet of three different houses and a garage, including the small house my wife had lived in before we got married.

"So why can't you do something about it?!"

"Well, here in Hillbilly Township[64] we can't make other people cut down their own trees," he explained. "We don't have ordinances about that." He looked back up at the tree. "Maybe we should?"

Much as with the debate over pets, there are at least two sides of the ordinance debate:[65] The "why-can't-you-do-somethings?" versus the "why-don't-you-leave-us-alones?"

For every deadly tree hovering over someone's house like the Sword of Damocles there's an equal and opposite healthy and leafy tree whose owner doesn't want anyone telling them to cut it down merely because the neighbor across the street doesn't like leaves blowing in his driveway.

Where to draw the line?

When that huge dead tree next to my wife's rental house finally fell that spring (just like she told them, she ordered me to type) and destroyed the fence, a corner of the neighbor's garage, their deck, their siding, a window and a sliding glass door, it seemed maybe the line had been drawn in the wrong place.

The tree caused no damage to our property. We enjoyed the unmitigated joy of a "told you so" moment with no consequences at all. The tree had conveniently broken off right above our fence-top level and plowed its massive furrow of destruction off to the north and west, away from us.

The retired couple with the adorable little lake house, the sort that has round windows and patterned field-

---

[64] Not the township's actual name.

[65] As the old saying goes: "There are two kinds of people in the world, those who divide every thing into two categories and those who don't."

stone landscaping, weren't so lucky. Besides the damage, detailed above, EMTs took the man of the house to the hospital because he thought he was having a heart attack. It took more than a year of fighting with their insurance company and contractors to restore their house to habitability. The corner of their garage still looks kind of wonky.

And the neighbor who owned the tree? The one with the dog-shit-filled yard who tossed cigarette butts over the fence? While everyone was out surveying the chaos this mullet-headed fellow ambled over to the end of the property, looked through the remains of his fence and said to the elderly couple, "Well damn! I guess that tree ain't my problem no more. Now it's yours!"

Litigation is pending.

The strangely tall and narrow house on the right is being built in Houston to cut off the sun shining on the solar panels of the older house on the left. Media stories labeled this a "solar spite house."

***

Ordinances exist to stop the criminally stupid from allowing dead trees to kill their neighbors. And to stop people like us from filling up our front yard with vintage pickup trucks we're going to fix someday, or with our collection of decorative cement gargoyles.

Some neighborhoods arguably need more such checks on a neighbor's freedom to burn household trash below your asthma-afflicted baby's bedroom window.

Other neighborhoods can seem slightly over-regulated when they measure the height of your grass from orbit and automatically email you a ticket.

How do you feel about that?

Whatever your position on the necessity of regulation isn't it odd that no one fills you in about such local ordinances before you buy a house?

Can you or your neighbors build a fence? Can it be built out of surplus pallets and cardboard? How about a tree house? A window box? Depends on where you live. Can you park your RV or boat in the grass next to the driveway? Is there a local leash law? Limit on the number, size and type of pets? Do driveways have to be paved, or is gravel ok?

Do you need a building permit for any of the above? Inspection? Is there a fee?

Ordinances (A Parable)

These rules very directly affect your quality of life.

They make a much larger difference in your life than granite counter tops or whether the downstairs bath has a single or double bowl sink.

Do you recall ever hearing of a real estate agent or home seller briefing a buyer on these relevant facts?

ORDINANCE PREFERENCES:

- OK to run chainsaws before 6am   __Yes __No
- Toilets as flower pots ok   __Yes __No
- Garage bands welcome   __Yes __No
- Creative house additions welcome   __Yes __No
- Cigarette butts, dead trees, fast food wrappers, dog poo responsibility of land they fall on   __Yes __No
- Can I keep toys entering my yard.   __Yes __No
- Neighbors okay with my taking their mail   __Yes __No
- Firearm discharge okay between 9 and 5   __Yes __No
- Code enforcement will measure my grass   __Yes __No
- Permit required for sidewalk use   __Yes __No
- Llamas must be leashed   __Yes __No

Nope. You won't find these check boxes in your real estate materials. Do you know why?

Because if anyone did bother to consider these issues your local real estate agent would end up doing many times more work to find you a house that really fit your life and made you happy.

Imagine the bizarre frustration: "This next house has a gas fireplace and two-car garage like you were looking for. Unfortunately, they have local ordinances that prohibit you from allowing your pack of yappy Chihuahuas to roam the neighborhood unleashed all night wearing glow-in-the-dark doggy tutus. And you won't be able to set up that authentic "bathtub Madonna" you inherited from your aunt. I know how much you hate fruit trees and orange colored cars, though, so you'll be happy to know both are prohibited. Um… how important is it to you that your neighbors not be allowed to walk in their yards during daylight hours? I'm having a tough time with that one."

What fun! Earn that $13,500, Gail®!

Instead, the house pushing industry just pretends none of these issues exist.

Nice.

But you can't ignore these restrictions on your life.

You've never seen a Bathtub Madonna?

Even if you want to live in the relatively-unregulated frontier of a "Hillbilly Township," there are a great many potential rules and regulations that will shape your life.

Some jurisdictions require you shovel the sidewalks within 24 hours of snowfall. Or be fined. Even if you're at your cousin's condo in Miami that week.

Others prohibit parking on the street overnight. Some municipalities pick up autumn leaves if you pile them at the curb. Others prohibit piling leaves at the curb.

Some require that you water your lawn, others prohibit sprinklers.

Won't it be fun finding out what rules now govern (or fail to protect) "your house?"

Home Owners Associations

> *"Individual stupidity can be remedied, but institutional stupidity is much more resistant to change."*   Noam Chomsky

If the petty, persnickety, authoritarianism of local ordinances bothers you then you might want to skip this section on Home Owners Associations completely. The Covenants, Conditions, and Restrictions (CC&Rs) of a HOA can make local ordinances seem all hippy-dippy and loosey-goosey by comparison. It's like the difference between going to the principal's office and going to a CIA Black Ops prison.[66]

Courts have upheld the power of HOAs to violate Constitutional rights and fundamental democratic principles because HOAs act as private actors contracting with house owners, not as governmental agencies.

As always, you're free to bargain away your rights.

In some states HOAs can foreclose on and sell your house to satisfy unpaid fines with no judicial review. HOAs can impose fees and special assessments and fines with little meaningful limitation. HOAs that act contrary to law or their own CC&Rs are almost impossible to bring into line.

HOAs are such amazing entities that this book isn't sure what to safely say about them. It doesn't seem

---

[66] The lesser known Fifth Horseman of the Apocalypse: private-sector authoritarianism.

possible to overstate how powerful, invasive, and dictatorial HOAs can be.

But if we tell it like it is, you the reader will likely think we have permanently donned a tin foil hat made from metal left over from 9/11 [Because, as you well know, jet fuel can't melt steel beams!]

So let's let the financial services industry speak for us: "One of every five Americans lives under rules and regulations that could confiscate their homes from them, remove their right to privacy and take away their freedom of expression. Neither Congress, the police nor local governments can do anything about it.[67]"

Whoa. Does sound dire, doesn't it?

> **Do you ♥ HOAs?**
> Well good on ya. This is a big book and we have room for everyone here. But before you decide to skip this chapter please pause for a second. Remember that no matter what you do, someone else hates it. HOA regulations (CC& Rs) can run to hundreds of pages and you would be a rare human indeed if they didn't restrict something you find important to your enjoyment of life. Or something you might wish to have as an option later. Any organization with that many rules will engage in "selective enforcement." That just means they follow some rules and ignore others. But the ignored rules still exist. Which means at any time your HOA might decide that the roses they allowed you to plant –the ones given to you by your dear late grandmother-- need to be destroyed. Stories abound of good citizens, rule followers, who woke up one morning to some Kafkaesque nightmare involving litigation or fines due to some violation of some rule they were not even aware of. Giving that much power to anyone for any reason is foolish and risky. Think about it.

"Fifty-five million Americans live in developments overseen by community associations," says consumer watchdog Ken Hyland. "Four out of five of those associations are doing well, but the other 20 per cent have problems."

Let's see. 20% of 55,000,000 that means there are at least 11,000,000 people in America with "problems" even worse than "living under rules and regulations that could confiscate their homes from them, remove their right to privacy and take away their freedom of expression" that "neither Congress, the police nor local governments can do anything about…."

Plus, wait, did that imply that giving up your Constitutional rights and being subject to random confiscation wasn't a "problem?" See what we

---

67 *"Homeowner Associations: Devils or Angels?"* http://www.bankrate.com

meant about the tin-foil-hat-sounding hyperbole?

If you'd like to spend some time online, you'll find many thousands of angry stories like this::

"*My brother "owned" (not really) a home governed by one of these Communist collective HOAs. They told him what kind of flowers he could plant, how long he could keep his garage door open, how often he could have his grandchildren for an overnight and how long they were allowed to stay, what paint colors he could use, how high he could have his lamp post, whether or not he could have numbers on his house so people could find him among all those boring, ticky-tacky buildings. They even put the squash on his selling the house, rejecting the prospective new buyer because he was 'not the right type' (the new buyer was black). Some fool even tried to tell him that his CAT was the wrong color and did not fit the community decor, and tried to force him to get rid of it. Finally he got smart and got out, despite taking a heavy loss.*"

In the 14 months we've been monitoring the media for noteworthy stories about HOAs we've become increasingly pessimistic about the future of humanity.

Each and every day we've found at least one heartrending story of a dying child, wounded vet, struggling single parent, grieving widow, or similar sympathy-eliciting house owner being victimized by an amazingly clueless and dictatorial HOA.

We're sorry but according to the HOA CC&R families are limited to the number of stick figures on the registered family vehicle. If you add another child you'll be fined.

But that isn't the most shocking and pessimistic part.

Each of these house owners voluntarily gave a HOA prison-warden-like power over every aspect of their lives.

In fact, to be perfectly accurate, each of them <u>pays</u> a HOA to limit their Constitutional rights and freedoms, family life, recreational activities and living arrangements.

This book could explore the question of why a seemingly sane family might spend around $1,000,000 over 30 years for a house, then pay an additional $150 per month to be told they can't fly a flag, decorate for Halloween, own certain animals, paint their house, host an exchange student, place election signs, grow vegetables, put up a hammock, allow their dying child a playhouse, or otherwise have the freedom to do most of the things people say motivate them to buy a house in the first place.

That would be a book about masochism, however, and this book is about why you likely shouldn't finance a house.

So in this book we will confine ourselves (much like residents of a HOA) to outlining reasons that spending your money to buy a house micromanaged by other people isn't such a great idea.

In The Beginning

How did the Land of the Free and Home of the Brave® spawn such a shackled, conformist, Stalinist, prison-camp mentality as HOAs?[68]

We'd hate to imply that today's HOAs were born out of hatred, bigotry and racism. So we'll just come right and say very clearly: HOAs were born out of a history of hatred, bigotry, and racism.

The ancestor of today's HOA bevy of rules was the "restrictive covenant." These were little contractual clauses that people placed into property deeds that mandated or prohibited certain uses of the property. Doesn't sound so bad in the abstract, but in the event these restrictive covenants were used mostly to prevent land from being sold to or owned by "undesirable" groups of people: the Irish, Jews (often identified in these contracts as "Hebrews"), Catholics (sometimes identified as "Papists"), African Americans (often identified in ways we won't repeat here), Non-protestants, Mexicans, Italians, Asians (often identified as "Japs" and "Chinamen"), Germans, Hungarians, Albanians, Communists, Baptists, "followers of Muhammad, or "Muselmen," Atheists, Indians, "Colored Peoples," etc. Pretty much every minority group was discriminated against by these clauses.[69]

> "If we sell one house to a Negro family… then 90 or 95 percent of our white customers will not buy into the community."
> - William Levitt, FHA-backed master builder of American suburbia and founder of "Levittown," the prototypical American suburb.

Eventually, the American government came

---

68 "Land of the Free and Home of the Brave" is a protected trademark of the NAR.

69 Because, apparently, that's what Americans wanted of their neighborhoods

along and declared that such restrictive covenants were unlawful, discriminatory, and prohibited. Kind of. Well. No. Actually, that isn't what happened at all. Instead the Supreme Court merely ruled that while parties were free to add restrictive covenants to private contracts, such private contracts were no longer enforceable by courts as that would violate the Equal Protection Clause.[70] You damn kids go ahead and do whatever you want, they were saying, but don't coming running to me every time you have a disagreement.

> One state government just passed legislation to address the crisis of unaccountable HOAs. Oh, wait. No they didn't. They are giving crooked HOAs more freedom and less accountability.
> *"It's important for homeowners to understand that their boards of directors, officers, and others may be already immune from liability and accountability to the association, even for gross negligence or other intentional acts that may be questionable. The new law shields the powerful few from possible legal repercussions at the expense of the many trusting homeowners who may be adversely affected by the almost imperceptible details buried deep inside the law."*
>
> (http://www.dbusiness.com/daily-news/Annual-2015/Guest-Blog-State-Legislature-Deals-Severe-Blow-to-Homeowner-Associations/)

Soon societal changes like Interstate highways, the widespread availability of cars, and the building of suburban developments controlled by private associations (rather than those pesky fairness-obsessed governmental entities) created fertile new opportunities for bigots.

Rich developers flocked to poor rural outlying areas and threw their weight around. Spurred by the massive housing shortfall after WWII and during the baby boom that continued into the 1960s, these developers created entire new communities out of former farms and forests.

Farmers, in their turn, discovered that it was often much more lucrative to grow houses than to grow corn. They often sold out and moved. Sleepy crossroads suddenly became towns. These towns suddenly had tax bases. And developers became amazingly wealthy and powerful building their little private-sector cities for people who wanted to move out of real cities.

Many of the people who wanted to move out of cities and into these little private fiefdoms were the very same folks who had tried to prohibit others from owning property under the now kinda-sorta forbidden restrictive covenants. So, guess what they were looking for in their new communities? (Hint: it wasn't diver-

---

70 <u>Shelley v. Kraemer</u>, 334 U.S. 1, 68 S. Ct. 836, 92 L. Ed. 1161 (1948), the U.S. Supreme Court held such covenants to be unenforceable in state courts because any such enforcement would amount to State Action in contravention of the Fourteenth Amendment to the U.S. Constitution.

sity.) Coincidently this was occurring *after* the Shelley v Kraemer decision (See footnote 67) but *before* the Civil Rights Act was working its way through Congress. Also coincidently, infamous Senator Joe McCarthy was heavily involved in the nod-nod, wink-wink shift of new housing to the racially charged, bigoted,

not-bound-by-all-that-fair-and-just-nonsense, private sector. Because of course he was.

Lucky for those who were seeking to discriminate, restrictive covenants might officially be kinda-sorta discouraged by our cowardly high court, but they were quietly alive and well in these sprawling new private sector enclaves.[71] As so often happens, the private sector was allowed and even encouraged to do what government is prohibited from doing by public pressure and that pesky Constitution and Bill of Rights.

To be fair, local governments found HOAs to be a blessing for other reasons. Of course, the reasons weren't very flattering. These additions to the tax base took care of many of the responsibilities previously left to the government: code enforcement, street maintenance, etc., so the local governments wouldn't have to do their jobs.

> "Curiously, with rare exceptions, when the State has notified boards of minimal association legal obligation to owners, they dispute compliance. In a disturbing number of instances, those owners with board positions use their influence to punish other owners with whom they disagree. The complete absence of even minimally required standards, training or even orientations for those sitting on boards and the lack of independent oversight is readily apparent in the way boards exercise control. Overwhelmingly (...) the frustrations posed by the duplicative complainants or by the complainants' misunderstandings are dwarfed by the pictures they reveal of the undemocratic life faced by owners in many associations. Letters routinely express a frustration and outrage easily explainable by the inability to secure the attention of boards or property managers, to acknowledge no less address their complaints. Perhaps most alarming is the revelation that boards, or board presidents desirous of acting contrary to law, their governing documents or to fundamental democratic principles, are unstoppable without extreme owner effort and often costly litigation."
> New Jersey Department of Community Affairs

Kinda sounds like the operating manual for a comic book villain's secret underground lair, doesn't it?

---

71 Further reading: http://usatoday30.usatoday.com/news/nation/2010-08-03-racistcovenants03_ST_N.htm; http://www.ibtimes.com/hoa-rules-why-it-necessary-home-buying-189538

In The Beginning

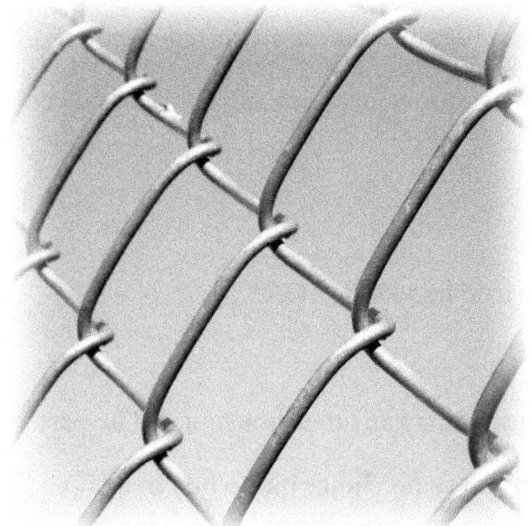

"We're all our own prisons, we are each all our own wardens and we do our own time. I can't judge anyone else. What other people do is not really my affair unless they approach me with it. Prison's in your mind. Can't you see I'm free?" *

HOAs accomplish this through double taxation. House owners pay property taxes like everyone else and they pay HOAs fees which act as additional taxes and fund services the local government no longer has to pay for. More money, less work. If you're a government, what's not to like?

Well, plenty, if you own a house in such a situation. Living under an HOA means you have fewer rights, less freedom, more costs, and almost no recourse against the HOA for shenanigans of which you don't approve. On the other hand, though, you gain a governing board empowered to sue people for selling Girl Scout cookies and hosting yard sales, and possibly willing to discourage "the wrong kind of people" from buying in.[72]

One of the most common types of news articles about HOAs involves spectacular corruption and malfeasance. Since HOAs are little quasi-libertarian-enclaves created through voluntary contracts, there's almost no real-governmental or regulatory or judicial oversight of HOA governing bodies. House owners agreed to give their HOA absolute power. Surprisingly, the people with all that power often end up abusing it.

HOAs embezzling money. HOAs funneling lucrative contracts to spouses, family members, or friends. HOAs spending ridiculous sums of money to punish some poor slob who painted her shutters the wrong color or planted a local high school spirit sign in the yard before homecoming. HOAs targeting and destroying the lives of residents they don't like for some other reason. It's terrifying. Do your own Google® search to discover the newest offensive and horrifying HOA scandal this week.

---

72 We don't want to give you the impression that HOAs are the *only* discriminatory housing entities. Your government and the finance industry can be equally bigoted. "*From its inception (the) FHA set itself up as the protector of the all white neighborhood. It sent its agents into the field to keep Negroes and other minorities from buying houses in white neighborhoods.*" Columbia Professor Charles Abrams, from <u>Housing and the Democratic Ideal</u>, released in 1955 discussing the ties between government racism ad the founding of American suburbia. This from more recent research by the Fair Housing Center of Greater Boston. "*Mortgage discrimination testing revealed differences in treatment that disadvantaged homebuyers of color 45% of the time. (FHCGB Audit 2005-2006)* "Upper income African Americans are 8 times more likely to have high cost loans than their white counterparts." "*The presence of high-risk lenders is 3.7 greater in minority neighborhoods than in white neighborhoods (Paying More for the American Dream, 2008)* "Upper and middle income African Americans and Latinos are 10 times more likely to have high cost loans that low income whites." (MA Community Banking Council)" These are random quotes. If you are interested there are entire sections of the library devoted to this stuff.

* (The photo caption, above, is from everyone's scary-crazy uncle, Charles Manson.)

In The Beginning

So far we've painted a pretty bleak picture of HOAs: authoritarian, obsessive, omnipotent, cruel, expensive, arbitrary, often providing a thin veil for racism and other bigotry, prone to excesses and abuse of power. So what's the upside?

"… chirp, chirp….tweet…. (sound of spring breeze blowing)"

No, seriously. Why do people voluntarily choose to live under the iron hand of a HOA?

Apparently there are three main reasons.

First, HOAs aren't always strictly "voluntary." In many areas of the country any new housing will be part of a HOA. If you want a newer house, or a house in a particular area, you've no choice but to buy in a HOA community. Governments have receded and allowed these HOAs to take over. A potential buyer has no choice except, of course, to choose to not buy a house.

Second, not everyone really "gets" the magnitude of issues with a HOA. Many people tend to think of HOAs as benevolent and supportive. As with local ordinances, most people know little about the reality of CC&Rs and most real estate agents don't provide much detail. Except positive spin. The house selling industry is invested in spreading that feel-good view. *"HOAs keep vampires at bay. You'll notice as we drive through you'll not see a single vampire!"*

Last, there are certain people who purposefully seek out these limited and restricted environments. These people are willing to limit their own freedoms in order to limit the freedoms of others. Which doesn't sound all bad. Within reason, that's kind of a good working definition of a representative Democracy. In this more extreme case, however, we're talking about something a few orders of magnitude more invasive.

We're talking here about the sort of person who is willing to put the nipple-clamps of real authoritarianism on themselves just to know that others are experiencing the same pain. In fact, these folks seem to derive real pleasure from experiencing such pain, and from mandating it for others. They're even willing to pay for this experience.

It makes you wonder if the real action in HOA communities isn't on the sterile, over-regulated, over-priced streets but, instead, is in the basement dungeons.

130   Open House: Debunking the Myth of the "Happy Homeowner"

"It's far worse than anybody suspects..."
Ward Lucas[73]

Chapter 4 take-aways.

- In real life people don't buy a house and live happily (and trouble free) ever after. Real people have real problems and financing a house usually makes those problems even more debilitating.
- Owning a house can, indeed, provide a feeling of happiness, but only to those who have already deluded themselves into believing that owning a house will make them happy. This works much like other personality disorders with clinical names.
- Buy a house and be as good as married to uncomfortably-close, potentially hostile strangers.
- Buying a house to escape problems is like using a credit card to pay off your gambling debts.
- Contrary to popular belief buying a house does not buy freedom. There are few in a free society as indentured and powerless as the owner of a financed house.
- Obtaining a mortgage can be compared to making a bargain with The Godfather, or entering into a fiddle contest with Mephistopheles: it may get you what you want but at a cost you don't (you can't) understand yet.
- Insurance is mandatory to finance a house and such insurance gives the carrier TSA/HSA/FBI-like authority over the house and its "owners" and occupants.
- Utility companies and the road commission and other entities exert stifling control over a house owner's property and are fond of passing this control on to random strangers.
- Local ordinances are cleverly designed to prohibit house owners from favorite activities while providing unpleasant people the tools to make everyone miserable.
- HOAs are all-powerful, scandal-plagued and unaccountable. House owners pay for these services.

---

[73] Ward Lucas is the author of *Neighbors At War*, a book about the horrors of HOAs. http://neighborsatwar.com/

Conclusion

Given that buying a house is the largest financial commitment most people ever make, it seems a bit odd that the purchase is usually entered into based on false assumptions, inadequate information and bizarre—even delusional—financial expectations.

Most people shuffle forward in a zombie-like daze on the path to house buying as if there were no other options available and being chained to a life-draining mortgage was the human equivalent of an infinite supply of zombie "braaaaains."

Why are the real facts about financing and maintaining a house so surprising when (to be frank) all the information in this book has been just sitting there (and mostly what we've done is pull it together for you and add snotty comments)? There was no initiation ritual, no scouring the depths of the "Deep Web," no dark-alley interviews with cloaked whistle blowers wearing masks. You can find most of this stuff yourself using Google®. Once the spell is broken, you can just listen to the nonsense spewed by the house-pushers and notice how carefully they dance around the facts. You can figure out the truth by what they don't say and how they don't say it. But only if you are listening.

Why aren't we listening?

Like most important questions in life there are many possible answers.

Maybe it's because for most people house owning isn't really a financial decision. House owning isn't really about living accommodations, either. Instead, house owning is a coming-of-age ritual shrouded in layers of myth and treated as inevitable even if tragic. The modern version of marching over the edge of the volcano to appease the gods of adulthood and maturity.

Maybe it's because the house pushers spend all that money persuading. Not just ads. Not just lobbying. Not just houses-as-American Dream in movies and TV. Not just cable shows dedicated to The Proposition that All People Need a House. But a total and complete cultural penetration like, well, like the sort of scary

Conclusion

total and complete penetration you might find if you actually were scouring the depths of the Dark Web or visiting one of those HOA S&M dungeons, if you know what we mean.

The Myth of the Happy Homeowner has reached a level of ubiquity few such unfounded beliefs ever reach: it is so prevalent we've stopped even seeing it.

Maybe it's because there's no acceptable cultural alternative to the 30-year-mortgage-house so most people don't even realize many better choices are available. The alternatives don't have the cultural cache of mortgaging your future in return for giving up many of your rights and freedoms and much of your income for decades. Parents, peers and friends might give you the raised-eyebrow if you explain your decision to forgo wasting a million dollars on a house in favor of real investments and a nice rental. "But you must appease the volcano gods," they might just as well explain, "or you will never transmogrify from a rental pupae to a fully mature mortgaged butterfly!"

Maybe it's as simple as acknowledging we've been successfully lied to by the largest and most powerful conglomerate of for-profit entities in America. From your cousin the real estate broker to the local big box home junk store all the way to Wall Street: a huge chunk of our GNP is house related. They make all the money; we take on all the debt and work. Not a bad system (for them) till we all wake up screaming and pulling mortgage tubes and insurance wires out of our bodies.

What do you mean I have a balloon payment due in two more years?

Maybe the Myth of the Happy Homeowner is a relic. An artifact left over from an earlier, simpler time when owning land and a house really was the key to building wealth and freedom. Maybe the myth is an echo from way back before the developers and brokers and title companies and finance companies and insurance carriers and resellers and HOAs and no-money-down window replacers figured out how to siphon off all the profit and leave us with only the debt?

Like most important questions in life maybe the answer really doesn't matter as much as the asking.

Another question: So what?

After 55,000 words debunking one of the most cherished and unassailable of American myths maybe your

Conclusion

So you mean... Maybe...maybe I don't *have* to finance a house?!?

reaction is to ask: "so what?" Like cable providers, dental drills and traffic lights, houses financing can seem just as unavoidable as it is unpleasant. Houses are expensive. They are the cause of frustration, anxiety, tedious labor and forgone opportunity. But that's the world we live in. So what? What choice do we all have?

The choices are almost infinite once the myth has been debunked. What choice do we have? Any choice we can imagine.

Pay rent and save the granite-counter-top money for a trip to the vineyards of Italy or the Indy 500.

If you must buy a house, wait four more years to polish that credit rating, save the 20% down, and go toe-to-toe with the transaction cost people till you find someone willing to make you a better deal on the selling and finance and insurance. If your parents are so damned determined that you buy a house ask them to loan you the money to buy it for cash and you can pay them back rather than carrying a mortgage. You'll save hundreds of thousands of dollars and force them to put some skin in the game. Maybe they'll suddenly discover that turning you into a happy homeowner isn't really that important to their life plans. Buy a fixer-upper for one third its market value and learn how simple and archaic house construction really is as you cut and hammer. Find a duplex, live in one half and rent the other.

Find a nice quiet apartment. Park an RV behind a friend's barn. Rent a room from someone. Get a self driving car and sleep in it as it cruises around town. Use the money you save to start a business or ride your bike across China.

Or.... Go ahead and finance a house. That's still an option too. Just don't wander naively into the project merely because you were told to do so, or because someone taught you that you aren't a grown up or a "real family" until you have a house. Don't buy a house thinking you are buying peace of mind. Houses are one of the largest responsibilities a person can take on and a house means decades of work and headaches, not "happily ever after."

Especially don't fool yourself into believing you are mak-

Like buying a house, it's an extravagance. But I'm worth it!

ing an "investment." Houses are luxury goods. An extravagance. An extra. A responsibility. You are buying that restaurant just because you are hungry. So plan and execute your house financing project just as you would any other luxury purchase. Buy that house with the same mindset you'd use to buy an expensive sports car or small aircraft: "sure it's a huge waste of money but I want it!" If you can afford the luxury there is nothing wrong with that. As long as you realize a house is not an investment.

Don't make the mistake of treating a very expensive indulgence as if it were a necessity.

Just that simple change in attitude and perspective might be enough to save you many tens or hundreds of thousands of dollars as you realize that, hey, you're not going to "make money" by installing a heated floor in the garage or an Internet-ready commercial gas range in your second kitchen.

Much of the foolish squandering of money we've ridiculed in this book stems directly from such rationalizations; people who want to indulge themselves hiding behind the myth and pretending they are being practical or have no choice in the matter.

As we said at the very beginning of the book, we don't have any vested interest in whether you buy a house or not. But after researching and writing this book we sincerely hope we've at least managed to make you think a bit about the process, the details and the long term.

Good luck!

***

Post Script

Hi. Your author has a confession to make: I'm a serial house owner.

But I didn't go about things the way most house buyers do.

I bought my first house on a land contract when I was just 24 years old. For more than two years I drove a truck, working two shifts, averaging about 75 hours a week while I lived in a ratty house trailer that cost $150 a month. It was a hole, the sort of place you can only find in rundown areas with no zoning or building codes, but I was never home anyway. That's how I saved up a 35% down payment and negotiated a ridiculously low interest rate (2%).

Within a month of closing I was spending all of my evenings, weekends and holidays destroying drywall and running wires. Within a season I had dropped back to one shift at work and torn off both porches and dug up the front yard to pour a retaining wall so the basement wouldn't collapse. A year in I quit the job to go back to college full time while I ripped off the entire existing roof line, added a shed dormer, two bedrooms, skylights and an upstairs bathroom. The following summer I completely renovated the downstairs bath, adding a vaulted ceiling and separate tub and shower with a skylight. I then replaced all the doors and windows, kitchen cabinets, carpet, and trim and painted every surface I could get my hands on. I sided both the house and the garage. Three years in there was almost nothing of the original house remaining.

I did all this while working two jobs attending college full time and juggling various other interests. I would come home at 10:30 at night, grab a sandwich and a beer, and begin disassembling walls or framing a closet. I had no spending money. My hands and arms were a constant mass of cuts and scars. I lost friends. My family never saw me. Girlfriends who stuck around long enough to form an opinion thought I was insane. Professors assumed I was a bouncer or drug dealer because I always looked sleepless and like I'd been in a fight. I recall one Christmas Eve spent on the roof, in the snow, with lights and tarps, working till well after midnight while my family was gathered around a fire.

Years later, in hindsight, I think I was mentally unstable. Or maybe I was just scared to death the house would win?

***

Tutoring on campus didn't pay well, so one summer after I bought the house I worked for the US Census to fund a new furnace and finish the upstairs bathroom. My scrapes and scars and generally unkempt demeanor apparently convinced the supervisor that I was a more suitable candidate for scary assignments than the room full of middle-aged housewives who were my fellow enumerators. So I got a pay bump and was assigned to prowl the sketchy rooming houses and tenements of a city that was–at that time—the "Murder Capitol of America."

Within a week I met the gentleman who now has the honor of being only the second person ever to point a gun in my face.

This armed citizen and I ended up having a nice discussion about his census statistics and sharing a malt liquor after he decided I wasn't enough of a threat to shoot, at least not that day. He confided in me then that his gun wasn't really loaded because loaded guns weren't allowed in the rooming house. My house owner skills came in handy: I helped him fix his door latch.

The rest of the summer was like that. I really earned my furnace money.

***

After the census gig ended, I landed a job working construction to bring in more much-needed cash and–I hoped—to learn a bit about the correct way to do all the house projects I was undertaking. In the days before YouTube how-to videos I had been relying upon luck, guesses, and random advice from friends and old guys at the lumber yard. I had spent a couple of frustrating days building a wall between what might someday become a bedroom and a bathroom if all turned out well. A worried thought led me to re-measure and discover I had built the wall two inches too far to the bathroom side. It wouldn't work. While I was pondering whether to give up, cry, or get drunk, a friend from the construction crew stopped by to check on my (in)sanity.

Peering at my misplaced wall, he asked me again which way the wall was supposed to move. I pointed. Setting down his beer[74] he picked up a sledgehammer and smacked the base of my wall, hard. It moved about a half inch, distorting the two nails I had used to hold it in place. "What's holding the top?" he pointed up. "Not much..." I started to say. He picked up the big hammer and smacked the top. A board splintered slightly but the wall moved a full inch.

He sat the hammer down and picked up his beer. "You aren't machining engine parts," he said. "You aren't doing brain surgery. It's just a house. Put away your micrometer. Houses are built like shit. Ease up a bit and just make it work."

---

74 Maybe you've gathered by now that beer is a very important part of owning and repairing a house.

Post Script

Construction jobs taught me a lot about how to build American houses: Cheap, quick and without sweating the small stuff. I also learned a lot about how the industry sees your "Dream Home."

During my second summer as a construction worker I was running a small crew finishing up some last minute detail work on a fairly large renovation. I found a few small problems that were not on my check list and I was in the middle of working them off when the boss showed up. He pulled me aside and explained why those obvious faults were not on the check list.

"Homeowners," he explained, "are stupid."

He paused, waiting for me to nod. "But they're spending a lot of money, so they don't want to feel stupid. They want to come in and nitpick and tell you how you ought to do your job. They think they could do it better, but they just choose not to. So they hire us "lowlifes" to do it. (The scare quotes were audible in his tone of voice)

He walked me over to a missing piece of trim I was about to install. "See that trim? You can spot it as soon as you walk down that hall. I don't want to say 'you can't miss it' because homeowners are stupid and you'd be shocked what they miss."

He pointed up at the trim. "But they will almost for sure see it. See how it's the end piece that's missing? Super easy fix. Take two minutes." He looked at me. "I left that off on purpose. For the homeowner to find."

He went on to explain that after every job, no matter how large or small, the homeowners would walk through and look at the work. And they would always find two or three things to complain about.

"If you button everything up tight for them, they just look harder," he warned. "Next thing you know they're second guessing where we put the window, or the color of the tile. Big jobs. Stuff that might take days to fix."

He pointed back at the missing trim, "But if you leave them little stuff to find it makes them happy. Guy will come in here tomorrow with his wife. One of them will notice the trim is missing, probably her. She will pull his sleeve and whisper to him that she found a mistake. She will demand he come and dress us down for it. So the guy will come in and talk to me. He will either be grumpy and shitty that we screwed up, or grumpy and embarrassed that his wife made him come and complain. I will make a big deal out of fixing it. I'll apologize. I'll threaten to fire one of you guys. I might even compliment them on their sharp eyes." He smiled. "Then it will take me two minutes to fix."

"See how this works?"

Post Script

I nodded. Indeed, I was beginning to understand about how houses are built.

***

The roommate I recruited so I could pay for a new roof woke me up early one Sunday morning to inform me that his moped had been stolen. Now he couldn't get to his crappy job washing dishes. Or to class on Monday. He was giving notice that he was planning to move back to his parent's house. I knew I couldn't make it without his rent. So I convinced him to stay if I could recover his moped.

By then I'd developed a pretty good feel for my sketchy neighborhood and harbored a suspicion of where I might find the missing moped. After dropping my roommate off at his job, I headed back to the projects.

Sure enough, I found the moped, surrounded by a group of teens who were noticeably not attending church that morning but were instead celebrating their new acquisition by passing around a plastic bottle of liquor.

Thinking quickly,[75] I roared up to the group in the car, blasted the horn, hopped out and shouted, "Hey! That's mine!" I ran over to the moped, turned to the closest teen and shouted, "did YOU steal this!!?!" He looked at my loud, rusty car, my dirty clothes, my beard, wild eyes, scarred hands and huge mop of uncombed hair and started walking backwards. "Nah, man," he said, "I've never seen it before."

As the group stared, I grabbed the moped and tossed it into the trunk of the car. Then I turned and screamed at the top of my voice: "AAaaaaaaaaAaaaagh!!!!" [76]

One teen looked like he might speak, so I stared at him, pointed, and screamed, "JESUS IS WATCHING YOU!!" Then I hopped in the car and drove home as quickly as I could without dumping the moped out of the trunk.

The roommate stayed. In fact, years later, he bought the house from me.

***

Which reminds me of a long story about the day that roommate, Bob, moved in.[77]

---

75 This is known in the writing biz as "sarcasm." I actually acted without thinking at all and am forever grateful I did not get shot and stuffed in the trunk of my own car and set on fire.

76 Not sure of the spelling. Google® wasn't helpful.

77 No this isn't his real name. He is all grown up, married and with a respectable job now.

Post Script

My first two roommates had moved out. One had transferred to another college and left to start a summer job in the new city. The other had dropped out of college and moved home to his parents out of state. It was summer. August, actually. The driest month of the year where I lived. My summer job had unexpectedly ended early. And most importantly of all, my application for a home remodeling loan had recently been approved. Our state offered home improvement loans for low-income house owners, and as a student I had qualified...partly because I didn't bother to tell them I was a student.

I had already concocted a plan to build a second story and was waiting for just the right time. With two more bedrooms and an extra bathroom I could more than double the rent I made each month from roommates. So this convergence of events [old roommates gone, dry month, school not yet in session, money available] awoke me one Saturday in August with a drive to "just do it."

It took most of the morning to cut the north-facing side of my roof into bite sized chunks with a chainsaw and Sawzall.* The first section was maybe six feet wide and the full 18 feet from the roof peak down to the eave. After the first section was sawn loose I had backed up my old pickup near the house, connected a rope from the top of the roof section [at the very peak of the roof] to the bumper of the truck, and attempted to flip the section off onto the ground by driving the truck forward.

I discovered two problems. The section was too large and heavy and the truck was too light: the truck lifted and tires just spun. Not good.

So I had cut the remaining roof sections quite a bit smaller. Long and narrow. Sort of like pieces of lasagna noodle made of shingles and wood. And while I was cutting I decided I'd needed to pull the truck up to the house next time, tie the rope to the front bumper, and back it away. The front of the truck was heavier, I

No, this didn't happen way back in the 60s. I was just really poor and bought old vehicles.

reasoned, and the tighter the rope became the more it would lift on the front of the truck and apply pressure to the rear drive wheels thus increasing traction. So I reasoned.

By the time I had readied the entire volatile, heart-stopping, Rube Goldberg contraption for another try, this time with a small section of roof, it was mid-afternoon and neighbors had begun to emerge from their houses to watch.

The rope was doubled with both ends fastened separately and securely to the very top of the roof line around what had until recently been rafters. The other ends were wrapped to the huge frame of my 1966 Ford pickup near the front bumper. I began to slowly back up. The rope tightened. The front of the truck began to lift a bit. I watched through the windshield as the roof section began to move slightly. It raised an inch or two, the truck began to struggle, then the wheels started spinning. Drat!

So I pushed in the clutch and the truck rolled forward, the tension on the rope pulling it back to where I had started. The roof eased back down into place.

I shifted the big three-on-the-tree into neutral, killed the engine and climbed out of the truck to take a look at the rope. Everything looked great at the truck end. A trip into the house and upstairs and onto a ladder reassured me that all was well at the other end too. The huge old marine rope was plenty strong enough for the job.

"Give her some gas," hollered my neighbor, 'Hoot,' a burly WWII vet with three missing fingers and a huge vegetable garden. My roommates and I had sort of adopted Hoot, hosing mold off his roof, helping repair the fence around his garden, and occasionally jump starting his ancient Buick. Hoot thought I was insane but was always there with moral support as I OJT'd on my house. "Keep goin'! You almost got 'er!" He was sitting in a lawn chair in his front yard with a can of Old Style.

See that paper in the window? That is a building permit. I was fully authorized to undertake this semi-suicidal project.

I waved and climbed back into the cab. This time I backed slowly until there was tension on the rope... then I dropped the clutch and hit the gas. The truck jerked backwards and as the tires began to spin the roof section lifted, and lifted, and tipped back 90 degrees and fell with a huge crash into the front yard about ten feet from the house. The rope fell slack. I stopped the truck, pulled it up out of the road and into my yard.

I opened the truck door to applause and whistling. Even the neighbors over in the projects were watching and hollering and applauding. One down, seven to go. I walked over to the house to make sure I hadn't caused any [unintended] damage.

It took until late afternoon to carefully pull the remaining roof sections off the house. After each successful pull I stopped the truck, inspected the front end, climbed into the attic to look for problems and repositioned the rope. A couple of times I had to break out the chain saw again. As I was working on the next-to-last section, a friend stopped by to visit. "Holy crap," he observed shrewdly, "you ripped the roof off your house!"

"Only the front half," I corrected him. "Would you go across the street and see if Hoot has an extra beer? It's about 90 degrees and this is kicking my ass."

"I brought beer," he replied.

"It makes Hoot feel involved if you ask him for a beer," I explained.

That next-to-last section went fairly well. It was at the very far end of the house and my rope was extended past a length where it felt safe. The longer the rope, the more it stretched. I had this worst-case-scenario in my head where the stretched rope would pull loose a big chunk of roof and launch it at my windshield like a 2" thick, 80 foot long rubber band. I was ready to duck for all the good that would do. But the roof section pulled free, if at a scary angle, and then smacked loudly into the front of the house before tumbling into the growing pile of debris on the ground. This prompted a "Ohhhh…. Ahhh… Owwwwww" reaction from my audience, like they were watching fireworks. No serious damage though and I knew I was going to install new siding anyway. I missed the windows. That was my primary concern.

The last roof section was the really large one I had failed to move that morning. All day I'd been debating with myself whether I should just go up and cut it into smaller sections, or take a chance and try to pull it off as it was. There was no longer anything for the sections to lean on so I was afraid I'd run into all sorts of problems if I tried to cut it now. It was evening now and I still had a couple hours' worth of work to do, coving up the top of my house with a tarp. I could run out of time.

"You feel like risking your life doing something stupid?" I asked my buddy.

"Well, I'm here, right?" He smiled.

We climbed up to the attic and surveyed the remaining section. My idea was to jack the roof section up and out using an auto jack and a long piece of 4 x 4. Once we had the top of the roof pushed out till it stood more vertically, it would take little effort for the truck to pull it out and off. I hoped. But someone needed to stay and keep an eye on this unfolding chaos. I really didn't want the jack, or the 4x4, or the roof section, to fall through the ceiling into the kitchen. That would be bad.

"Please don't fall through the ceiling into the kitchen," I asked my buddy. "That would be bad too."

"No shit," he agreed amicably.

The plan worked, eventually, even if nothing like we hoped. My buddy, fortified with a sense of invulnerability at my insane success, and a few of Hoot's Old Styles, stuffed a large board into the space between the moving roof section and the standing wall. So when the rope broke the roof didn't fall into the house, or even back to its previous location. It ended up wedged eight inches in the right direction.

"Well that was stupid," I observed. "You could have gotten your arm ripped off or your head crushed in. Good idea though."

"You're welcome," he acknowledged. "Help me get some more boards in there."

On the second try the roof section pulled over and away and into the yard. This one was over twice as large, and twice as heavy, as the others. It fell awkwardly and smacked into a fence, and another section, crashing and spraying chunks of wood and pieces of shingles like an explosion. This prompted the biggest loudest round of applause yet from the audience. Many of them had chairs, now, too and most of them had beer. There were even people in my yard now. More than two dozen people had gathered around to see me destroy my roof. The fun now ended, they started packing up to go home.

After driving over and grabbing a burger and resting up a bit, my friend and I tackled the next project; covering up the top of my house with tarps I'd borrowed from a construction job.

We finished just as darkness was falling. The audience had long since dispersed except for Hoot who was still in his chair, joined now by a few empty Old Style cans. I thought he was napping but he yelled over and wished us well and disappeared into his house. We went inside to explore new and better beer. About 11:30pm there was a loud knock on the door. It was a uniformed police officer.

"This your house?" he asked.

"What's left of it," I joked. Ha. Ha. I had been drinking beer and had a very tough day.

Apparently it wasn't obvious to the officer, after dark, what I was referring to so the officer just looked puzzled. "Are you Jesse?"

I admitted that I was and waited to see what was to come. Was I in trouble for ripping off my roof? For dumping three or four tons of roof debris in my front yard? For endangering the public? Why was he here?

"Do you know Bob Harris? He says he lives here," the officer paused. "Sometimes."

Seems my friend Bob had gotten kicked out of another apartment and decided to set up camp in the local nature preserve. He was kinda-sorta living in a tent in the woods and kinda-sorta living in his car. This evening the nice police officers had run out of patience and rousted Bob and told him he was never, ever allowed to enter the nature preserve again. In lieu of going to jail he had told them he did have a place to go: he "lived" at my house. So—rather than have to arrest him—they agreed to drive him over. He was way, way too drunk to drive himself.

The house was only like this for a week or so. The view from the living room was amazing.

They managed to get Bob out of the car, dropped a duffel bag of his belonging on my porch, and my other friend and I got him to the couch. I'm not sure he ever really woke up. The officers left. We had another beer and called it a night.

The next morning, a bit late the next morning, I pulled the tarps off to let the sun air out the mess and went down to the kitchen to make some food, and some plans. I needed to start building a second story and a roof and have that all finished before the weather turned. Standing in my kitchen with the bright, unfiltered sunlight streaming through the space where I used to have a roof, I was beginning to wonder if the abrupt roof removal had been such a great idea.

While I was cooking eggs and bacon Bob woke up. He groaned a bit and turned over. He laid on the couch for a few minutes and said, "I can see birds flying around up in the sky?"

I looked up from my cooking, While the kitchen still had a ceiling, and a covering of plastic to keep things clean, there was nothing but blue sky above the couch where Bob lay. Birds were flying overhead.

"Yep."

"Is that you?"

Post Script

"Yep. One and the same."

A few seconds later. "And you are cooking…bacon?" Bob moved his head and looked around. "And… uh… is this the ratty gold couch from your house? I'm lying on your couch?"

I assured him that he was right on both counts.

So he sat up and looked at me through layers of pain and fog and asked, "So why the hell are you cooking bacon out here in the woods, and how did your couch get here?!"

***

Another day I decided to burn some scrap wood in a sort of makeshift bonfire. The sort of scrap wood that might include some shingles and other stuff I wasn't really supposed to be burning. The sort of stuff I could not afford to have hauled away in the volumes I was accumulating it. Since we had to sit and monitor the burn, me and a couple of buddies, who had generously donated their day for another one of my ridiculous remodeling projects, were hanging out in lawn chairs, watching the fire, having a beer. That's when we heard sirens. I immediately knew, somehow, that the sirens were because of us.

Apparently our little fire was so out of line that we had scared the nice folks in the public housing project across the field. The previous New Year's Eve I had watched residents of this same scrappy, rough and tumble housing project firing AK47s into the air and detonate homemade fireworks.

These were folks who tossed used diapers over the 8 foot high chain link fence and hung bags of used hypodermic needles on trees. My moped-stealing neighbors.

But on that particular day they had dodged gunfire and crackheads long enough to call 911 because of my DIY house project bonfire.

The very professional and amazingly patient fireman in charge of the truck spent about ten minutes making clever and insightful observations about my lack of intelligence and general irresponsibility. He helpfully pointed out that I had not only risked burning down "the entire f***ing neighborhood" but had wasted the time and resources of all these very irritated firemen.

He then observed that we were doing a great job fixing up the old house and that it was really inspiring to see someone trying to bring back the neighborhood. Apparently we were the talk of the town. Some of the other firemen chimed in: Good for us!

But, he wanted to be clear, if I ever pulled a stunt like this again his entire fire crew was potentially ready to beat my ass and then watch my whole damned house burn down. They did note, however, that we were

Post Script

being very responsible by having two garden hoses nearby to control the fire.

Then they left. They didn't even make us put the bonfire out. Seriously mixed messages. So we tossed more scrap on the fire, collectively offered a middle-finger salute to our shit-tossing neighbors in the projects, and opened more beer.

Two months later I persuaded my gainfully-employed brother to help me buy a second house. It was abandoned, condemned, and we picked it up so cheaply he put it on a credit card.

This house was bad. Really bad. We ended up pulling down all of it except the cement block walls and basement. We started completely from scratch. Just as winter began.

Houses: I was hooked.

***

I walked into that second purchase knowing that owning a house isn't anything like an episode of *This Old House* or *Remodeling Brothers*. No full crew or fancy shop stuffed with state-of-the art equipment. No sunny days free of obligation spent happily nailing and fitting high quality, custom-purchased material perfect for the job at hand.

Like everything else that sounds too good to be true, the fairy tale you heard about making money by just sitting home, paying the mortgage, and watching Netflix really isn't true.

Instead, house owning for profit is all about fitting filthy, demanding projects into free time, using the tools you've got on hand, making things work, and trying to use building material you get for free or on sale. Finding house money wherever you can scrape it up.

Cutting corners. Missing out. It's a job.

One day you wake up and realize you never contemplated dumpster diving for scrap lumber before you owned a house. You never planned vacations around "good building weather." You never tried to trick friends into "stopping by" so you could borrow a strong back to lift a shower stall. And you likely never considered selling plasma for a bay window or getting guns pointed at you to buy a furnace.

Is this how you picture owning a house? Does this at all resemble the "American Dream" painted for you by the house pushers?

I've had five houses now. And, sure, let's be honest. My experiences are not all that typical. That's one of the reasons I'm the guy writing the book: I've been to the far side and returned to tell my sordid tales. And, as this book keeps stressing, maybe the most atypical part of my experience is that I didn't lose money on my houses.

Most anyone who has owned a house can tell a story or two that will cause you to raise your eyebrows and make you second guess the idea of house ownership. Ask someone about their house-owning disasters. You might be shocked.

***

For most of us, a house is the largest purchase we ever make. Houses represent years of income. A house can be the difference between financial security and a life of scraping by and doing without. Houses have caused divorce, prompted bankruptcy, ruined businesses and even motivated suicide. Much of this book may be funny, but letting unexamined myths and unrealistic expectations about houses ruin your life isn't funny at all.

***

The day my father died I didn't get home until almost midnight. No end of unpleasant but necessary things to do at the hospital. Home was now a nice big suburban place located in one of the best school districts in the state. Lucky the place was large because I was hosting a house full of upset, grieving relatives including my mother, who was understandably not dealing well with the situation and had been physically ill for days.

> **The Scorpion and The Frog**
>
> A scorpion and a frog meet on the bank of a stream and the scorpion asks the frog to carry him across on its back. The frog asks, "How do I know you won't sting me?" The scorpion says, "Because if I do, I will die too." The frog is satisfied, and they set out, but in midstream, the scorpion stings the frog. The frog feels the onset of paralysis and starts to sink, knowing they both will drown, but has just enough time to gasp "Why?"
>
> Replies the scorpion: "It's my nature..."

It was early spring and a dreary rain had been falling for days. I headed into the basement to fetch a couple of beers for my brother and brother-in-law and stepped into four inches of icy standing water.

It took the three of us until 4am to pump out all the water and install the backup sump pump I had luckily bought cheap at an estate sale and stashed nearby. At 6am I was at the home improvement store buying a second sump pump and PVC pipe. By 9am I had two pumps installed in parallel, wired to different circuits, and a water alarm. Just in time to get cleaned up and start making funeral arrangements and facing life without my father.

Even the nicest houses have a way of kicking you dead in the crotch. They can't help it. That is their nature.

***

Post Script

I walked into my first house with a thousand yard stare, focused like a laser on one goal: I planned to make money. I was well aware of the nature of what I was doing. I had planned my moves carefully for a couple of years. So I approached the project with my eyes wide open.

In six years I more than quadrupled my investment. Using the sort of cold, calculating, no-BS accounting I've shared in this book. I counted every nickel. Each switch cover and board. Every trip to the landfill. All the money spent on interest and taxes. I filled the place with roommates to help pay the bills. I rented out storage space in my big garage. Each month I made more money than I spent. My house *created* income. It was not an expense.

Think differently or just avoid the hell out of ~~scorpions~~ houses.

I did not have a mortgage. Or PMI.

I made money. But I treated it like a job.

Are you prepared for a second job in your house? Ready to clock in and do your shift?

Or do you envision only the fun/easy parts?

Do you assume by just having a mortgage and paying the bills on time you'll magically accumulate vast wealth while living your normal life?

You won't.

Are you okay with spending, and losing, from 3 to 5 times the purchase price of a house just so you can pee on that fire hydrant and "make it your own?" Or, do you understand and accept the sheer life-changing magnitude of tackling a house that will "make money?"

If not, then you should stop and reconsider.

Broken Fourth Wall Note

At this point the authors of this book have read thousands of stories about "that neighbor" while searching for some that would entertain you and make this book more informative. Thanks to everyone for these stories. They've depressed us and ruined our faith in humanity.

Since we've acquired these soul-deadening tales on your behalf, after reading more of these stories than you'll likely ever hear, we thought we'd share some of our observations. After all, remember what G.I Joe used to say.[78]

Almost all of these stories we were told (most didn't make it into the book) fell into one of six broad categories:

1) Stories about people who are actually mentally ill.

You won't be seeing these stories in the book. Not only does it feel morally a bit contemptible to make fun of mentally ill people, further, for the purpose of proving a point, they are low-hanging fruit. A mentally ill person is acting in a potentially inappropriate fashion? No kidding. What point does that prove about owning a house?

2) Stories about people who are not neighbors but just oddballs encountered during life.

Town drunks. The homeless. People who walk or bike or skip or dance down the street wearing a tutu or ghillie suit, riding a unicycle or playing a tuba or wearing only a thong and a funny hat, but don't live next door. You won't find stories about these folks in the book, either. Not because some of them aren't hilarious, but because we're trying to demonstrate oddity and fear right next door where you can't escape it. We'll stick to stories about folks running a meth lab in the garage next to a kid's treehouse.

3) Stories involving pets.

These come in two standard flavors. First we have people with pets who are outraged that a neighbor doesn't love that person's pack of sweet, fuzzy little Rottweiler's and their non-stop barking, or large herd of screeching semi-feral cats, or the rooster they keep in the garage. In the other corner we have people who hate their inconsiderate neighbors' obnoxious (out of control, noisy, dangerous, destructive, unlawful wildly-pooping) pets. Some of these stories are hilarious and so are included in the book.

The best part of these particular stories is that they remind us that we're all "that neighbor" to someone.

---

[78] Knowing is half the battle!

4) Stories that center on property disputes or parking.

Reading these stories it can seem like there really are no grown-ups when it comes to property and parking disputes. Each of these storytellers defends her or his perfectly rational decision to toilet-paper the neighbor's house, or key the car, or toss dog poo on theiroof, while in the same breath denouncing their unreasonable and childish neighbor for making similar attacks on them. He cut my branch! She let her leaves blow in my yard! They park in the spot near my house on alternative Tuesdays when everyone is supposed to cross the street and park facing the other way! Screw all of these people. But if their story was funny enough, it was included.

5) Stories that could've happened to anyone, whether they own a house or not.

This book is about the trials and tribulations of owning a house. Oftentimes, if your neighbor is a pig, or an idiot, it doesn't really matter unless you actually own a house nearby. Those quiet people at the end of the street who hate living things and poisoned their lawn and cut down all their trees? That might infuriate you if you own a house near enough to suffer property devaluation, or escape your attention completely if you're renting. As we have exhaustively demonstrated, people who own a house are already losing money faster than they can keep track of it. They're not interested in watching property values and resale potential decline because some weirdo has defoliated their lot. Other stories concerned apartments, or wacky roommates. Still funny. But not relevant.

6) Stories concerning drugs, alcohol or illegal activities.

Some of the very best stories feature drunks or people engaged in unlawful activities. We consider drunks and criminals fair game. We stand in defense of these stories and their role in helping us make valuable points.

Other common bad neighbor stories involve:

Noise. Neighbors who like to mow or vacuum at 6 in the morning, or play drums or tuba until 2am. Or who call the cops at the sound of you closing your mailbox.

Neighbor's lifestyles and personal choices. "Too many kids!" "Fussy old people with nothing to do!" "Christmas decorations up in July!" "Weird Scientology®©™¶§[79] people with a big spaceship shaped altar on the deck!" "They refuse to participate in Trick or Treat and block their driveway with land mines!"

---

[79] Can't be too careful with the litigeous Scientology®©¶§™ types.

One last observation. A remarkable (and disturbing) number of people with bad neighbor stories volunteered gleefully that they were the problem neighbor. "Mom is a violent drunk," or "my brother sells pot out of his basement bedroom all night," or "my wife is the one who calls the HOA on people she doesn't like and makes up reasons," or "I always drive across their lawn when I know they're not home."

So in addition to the risk you take buying a house next to Jeffrey Dahmer or someone auditioning for a part in Jackass, keep in mind that you also face a small but significant demographic of neighbors who pride themselves in making other people's lives miserable. They brag about it.

Chances are that if you buy a house in a typical neighborhood you'll get stuck with at least one of these asshole/antisocial/pot-stirring neighbors.

Or maybe one like me.

Even after all these years I'm proud of that scary little hillbilly project. Look at the plane of those rafters. Perfect! Certainly the best built part of that old house.
But I'm pretty sure I was "that neighbor."

www.ingramcontent.com/pod-product-compliance
Lightning Source LLC
LaVergne TN
LVHW061311060426
835507LV00019B/2098